INTERDEPENDENT
ECONOMY

INTERDEPENDENT ECONOMY

✦

From Political Economy
to
Spiritual Economy

Liem Giok In

iUniverse, Inc.
New York Lincoln Shanghai

INTERDEPENDENT ECONOMY
From Political Economy to Spiritual Economy

iUniverse books may be ordered through booksellers or by contacting:

iUniverse
2021 Pine Lake Road, Suite 100
Lincoln, NE 68512
www.iuniverse.com
1-800-Authors (1-800-288-4677)

Cover design by Marc Susan, Art Photography & Design

ISBN-13: 978-2-595-33152-9(pbk)
ISBN-13: 978-0-595-77937-6(ebk)
ISBN-10: 0-595-33152-1(pbk)
ISBN-10: 0-595-77937-9(ebk)

Printed in the United States of America

INTERDEPENDENT ECONOMY

—from political economy to spiritual economy—

The term spiritual refers to the profound truth that all phenomena exist in an interdependent way only. No phenomenon exists in itself. All phenomena—animate or inanimate, mind or matter—come into being and cease to be by a constant flux of causes and conditions. In the process the one has an effect on the other and the other on the one. Therefore, if we desire happy states, we should create positive causes and conditions. It is *our own mental force* that creates all... and through which God's purpose manifests.

Homage to my precious teacher, Geshe Rabten Rinpoche, who sustained me in all my lives, sustains me in this life, and will sustain me in all my future lives.

With gratitude to the Congregation of the Ursulines with whom I lived from age one to two. Their love of God and love of the world have deeply nurtured my development.

"May all races live in harmony...
May Your Spirit come with new solutions...
May there be peace in the world..."
Were their words of prayer.

This book stands on the long-time and in-depth efforts of many researchers, activists, and others who, individually or through organisations, work for the socio-economic rights of their people. I acknowledge the great value of their words and actions, often done at the cost of personal sacrifice and against all odds.

Contents

Preface

I studied economics at an institute of some repute with industry, the University of St. Gallen, Switzerland. They taught me economics of course, but also I was told that by virtue of this education I now had joined the ranks of an elite that was to lead society. I was eighteen and smiled at this, in my opinion, empty claim. To govern others, I thought, required more than just to study matter. Not urged by any professional ambition, but by a thirst for inner knowledge, I embarked on a life-long path of Buddhist practice at the age of twenty-two. And here I learned that suffering permeates us all, both poor and rich.

When I was forty-four, I worked, earning very humble wages, for a vision called Gender Equity and International Cooperation held by a group of women and men wanting to influence policy. At this job, it was not so much the imbalance within gender that made me think, but the incongruence between economic policy and the economic needs of people. Incessant and heart-breaking were the many realities I had to read—for I was editor-in-chief of texts written in critique of policies. These policies, so I observed, were incessantly ignorant and arrogant when asked to take these realities to heart. Of course, for decades now there exists this ever-widening sector of protest and despair. And as a consequence, conservation of nature, protection of human rights, and poverty eradication are now themes declared to be "on the agenda." But looking at things precisely and on worldwide scale, can we say that the protest hit the policies and despair has turned into hope? I don't think so.

I am over fifty now and have written this information pamphlet. It tells us about things that are, for not knowing that what should be clear must be dealt with first. And if some among the readership could also act to change the course of policy along the lines of these proposals, then that would be the golden trophy that this paper hopes to win. I speak to all, to public and policymaker, to left and right, to South and North.[1] I blame no one, but are we not all responsible? We of

---

1. In Development Cooperation these terms denote the developing (South) and the developed (North) countries.

this elite rank who are endowed with the capacity to have our say on governance and with the freedom of thought to do it well.

Liem Giok In
Den Haag, March 2005

Introduction

What nowadays we call economics—thinking about the inherent laws of the economy and making conclusions about the best way to secure our wealth—was called *political economy* in the times of Adam Smith. He was, in the eighteenth century, one of the founding fathers of economic thinking. His voluminous and beautiful work *Inquiry into the Nature and Causes of the Wealth of Nations*[1] indicates that the procurement of life's necessities in the nations and societies he describes had become so complicated that it required deeper thinking to understand its processes. Why do we want to understand the economy? It is because we want to rule out insecurity; we want to take all measures possible to safeguard the undisturbed continuation of our basic livelihood as well as the further growth of our wealth. What does this word "political" indicate? It seems to indicate that there are agents who reflect on the *governing* of the economic processes for the good of the whole, rather than for the good of only one individual. Such agents can be big or small, with authority or without, and anywhere on the scale from pure-thinking to very operational. But typically, it is governments and their advisors that are the most visible agents of political economy.

In this book, I bring up the topic of economics from the point of view of one who wishes to plan the economy for the larger good; this discipline is called macroeconomics. Since times of old, students have been taught about the two distinct fields of *micro-*and *macro*economics. So these terms reveal no great new insight. The reason why I bring this forward here is because I believe that laws and logic that make sense in microeconomics are often uncritically transferred to the field of macroeconomics. This book will explain how that happens, and why it is not correct. More importantly still, this book will explain the *distinct* laws and logic of macroeconomics. It is these that should serve as the base for macroeconomic policy and planning, and therefore it is these that should be known and

---

1.   Adam Smith (1723–1790) was a Scottish philosopher. His *Wealth of Nations* was published in 1776.

1

understood by the men and women who have taken upon themselves the responsibility for the good of the whole.

Furthermore, this book is written for the well-being of all. In present times we all feel the effects of one interdependent economy on our lives. Production factors,[2] production, distribution, and consumption in the economy of today are globally interwoven. The threading of this global cloth links people and societies of different cultures and value systems, of different levels of worldly power and complexity of their economies. As leaders and institutions with global responsibility and influence practice their political economy, it is important that these differences are being recognised and all the positive aspects of the manifold cultures remain unharmed—for human plurality is the real richness of our world.

The spiritual economy that is being outlined here understands the structural poverty of the one society as factored by the over-development of the other. Or, in other words, spiritual economy recognises the interdependent nature of our economies and the effect of the policies of the one on the other. Thereby it wishes to take care of the whole.

Finally, this book will not only give an outline of concepts and views but will also give some initial suggestions for implementation.

---

2.   Production factors are, for instance, raw materials, land, labour, finance, or knowledge.

PART I
OUTLINE OF CONCEPTS AND VIEWS

When we say "macroeconomy" we can think of either theory or policy. Macroeconomic theory is the study of the relationship between the aggregated behaviour of economic agents (e.g., consumers, entrepreneurs) and economic entities (e.g., income, export volume, interest rate). The conclusions derived from these studies provide policymakers with the instruments to achieve their aims. Here, interdependent economy does not so much discuss theories, but thoroughly reconsiders policy aims. From this, new contexts for the development of theoretical models may ensue. However, for now I leave that subject matter by the side and attempt to penetrate into the practical foundations of macroeconomic policy.

1. Macroeconomy—Is It about Growth?

Since Adam and Eve were ousted from the Garden of Eden it became necessary for mankind to toil for its survival. The fulfillment of needs of livelihood was no longer something that could be expected to happen spontaneously, but had to be worried about.

It seems to be a forgotten theme nowadays, but the real raison d'être for all economic thinking and activity is the fulfillment of needs. Growth[1] seems to have won the prime place as the all-important trophy for economic policymakers and thinkers, with "stability" and "employment" in second place, and "free trade" as its loyal partner. We may have tremendous growth rates, fine stability, and full employment, but if people have to go without their basic wants being fulfilled, then the policies have failed. Sadly, this is the reality for many in our world.

And what about free trade? It can make or break people's lives, depending on so many relative and interrelated conditions. To proclaim free trade as the holy grail for which any knight of economic policy should be eternally searching is the greatest simplification of all times. The harm done by the dogma of free trade to millions of lives is in sad contrast with its high status with present-day national and international centres of power.[2]

This simple rearrangement of words—and thereby priorities—may seem to be futile. However, to consistently pursue the fulfillment of needs of livelihood as

---

1. "Growth" as it is critically discussed in the context of this book is understood as the increase of the economic output *over* population increase, that is, the output of more goods and services per person. Economic growth equal to population growth results in stable economic output/per capita rates and is needed to maintain existing standards of living.

2. The main thrust of trade negotiations nowadays is the opening up of national markets for foreign goods irrespective of the effects on people's livelihoods. One could, however, also organise world trade from the point of view of a sensible sharing of markets and industry among all nations that would ensure earning opportunities for all.

the outcome of all economic planning—rather than growth—will turn a very large part of policies completely upside down. Take the example of development projects like the building of (mega)dams,[3] meant to further growth. Projects like these have displaced millions of people to a life of nothing and nowhere. At the same time, promised benefits like electricity, irrigation, and drinking water materialise at only very small percentages of the initially planned volumes and benefit only a small group of people. The main beneficiaries from these projects seem to be the dam builders and the financial institutions, while the debt burdens that invariably trail behind these projects ruin any hope for future development for the people of the land. Nevertheless the projects continue and one cannot help wondering what the logic behind such policies is. Pressure from industry groups and corruption in politics cannot sufficiently explain such enormous economic failures. Deeper problems of failing cognition must be at work here.

What is this obscure failure of cognition that makes such ludicrousness persist? It is the power of a truth that we all seem to believe in. This truth is called "growth." It is a truth, indeed, from the point of view of the micro-unit: one individual, one family, one enterprise, one nation even, but it is not true from the perspective of macroeconomic policy.

Macroeconomics is about *the fulfillment of needs of people* in the context of many individuals functioning in an interdependent economy. All we have to ask ourselves when making a plan is: does this activity fulfill the needs of beings while not harming others? Growth may be a part of planning but should not be the primary lead for policy. Stability and full employment cannot be planned directly. They are the result of a multitude of variable factors plus their interdependent effects, which also bring in the factor time. No mathematical model, however complex, can ever catch that reality. This explains the well-known fact that forecasts by economic models are wrong by rule, and sometimes are correct by sheer luck.[4] The world's many interrelated aspects are unpredictable. But to pursue balanced policies that stem from a balanced view is a choice that we can make. To

---

3.   Thousands of these dams have been built and continue to be built in developing countries, although in industrialised countries these constructions have been already declared obsolete and environmentally damaging. See Appendix A on "Dam Projects in India and Tibet".

4.   Paul Ormerod, *The Death of Economics,* (London, 1994). In this book the author, who was formerly director of economics at the Henley Centre for Forecasting, describes the crisis in the "science" of economics. "Despite its powerful influence on public life, its achievements are limited as those of pre-Newtonian physics", so he says.

fulfill the needs of livelihood of people first is the view of an economic policy that will balance economies best.

Mathematical models as such do not give us a good economy. They can be supportive instruments. But what we need to do first is to weigh well what the real needs of people are. A fairly simple task for simple economies, but surely, when we deal with complex economies planning with the help of computed models may be necessary. What does not work, however, is to plan (promise) future fulfillment while not addressing present needs. So-called "trickle-down policies"[5] are no part of true planning. Such policies are typically heralded by those who themselves are at the top and therefore do not have to wait for the benefit to trickle down to the bottom.

5.   Trickle-down policies are policies that say to effect development for the poor by favouring corporations and top-income classes without at the same time putting in place policies that favour the poor. It is assumed that the gains of the rich will eventually trickle-down to the poor. Such policies have been widely preached and practiced by neo-liberal policymakers from the 1970s onwards. Their ineffectiveness has been established again and again and has been amply documented. Nevertheless, they still persist.

2. Successful Economies—An Example to Be Followed All over the Globe?

But how can we doubt the efficiency of presently applied policies that go by the hallmark of growth rates, those monetary measures that are followed with scrutiny year after year by politics and public alike? So many success stories are told by modern states that have become rich and powerful and by citizens that have increased comfort and consumption to levels beyond what they can digest. Is it not just a matter of extending the same policies to these hapless countries that due to all kinds of lack and limitations have not yet implemented the success formula? This formula is, of course, what is the mainstay of present-day international economic policies: helping the poor countries to the same programme of growth and stability, while fulfilling the basic needs of people is downgraded to an outcome hoped for at best, or not really cared for at worst. Obviously the logic here is what works for one part of the world, also works for the whole world. Or in other words, the micro-logic of nations—national growth is good for my nation—is uncritically transferred to the macro-situation of the whole world, of all nations together.

The micro-logic of growth, however, is by definition powered by the instinct for survival of the one unit. This implies the destruction, exploitation, or, at least, the neglect of others. It is impossible to say that this is wrong or immoral. It is just a law of nature, and it is the vigour of our existence. A nation that wants to grow will by definition exploit another, just as weeds that want to grow will destroy other plants, or one animal that wants to survive will chase another away from its territory or even eat it. It is impossible to apply the micro-logic of growth to each and every nation and people of this world and at the same time not to harm any nation or people. To solve this riddle we must either find planets in outer space to exploit or we must change the logic.

This reality may be hard to accept for many who live comfortably in places of ever-growing economies. They will think, "we never wanted to harm anyone and in fact we spend much intellectual energy in thinking how to help the world." How laudable this thinking may be—and this book hopes to meet many people who make efforts in this way—the mere wish not to harm anyone does not eliminate the mechanism by which harm is done. And a mechanism it is. Merely replacing a few clogs or screws will not do, the machine must be re-programmed. We must aim *directly* at the fulfillment of needs of people, not hope that it will be an outcome of growth policies.

Harming many by the growth of some is not only a story of the past—of colonial exploitation and slave trade—but very much of today. From the micro-logic of growth follows the logic of cost reduction and profit-maximisation. Again, this logic fits naturally the one unit, but see what it does to the whole—when all the interdependent units follow their instinct. What we see is the exploitation of cheap labour, the imposition of inhuman labour conditions, raw materials and energy resources being taken without paying the proper price, damage done to man and nature, disruption of local markets by global imports, trading—arms or diamonds[1]—that turns profit into destruction, massive amounts of working capital meant to serve people's basic needs transferred to banks of others whose basic needs are already fulfilled, and wars that secure the economic growth for some while killing life and hopes of others.

The micro-instinct, which serves the micro-unit well, just does not have the same life-preserving effect when applied to the whole. When interconnected by the strategy of interdependent economy growth policies can provide the dynamism for a balanced whole. Growth policies alone will not lead to world peace.

---

1. For instance in Angola and Sierra Leone the export of diamonds finances the war. International trade policy could ban such trade temporarily. For Angola see: http:// www.africaaction.org/docs98/ang9812.htm. For Sierra Leone see: http://gbgm-umc.org/umcor/emergency/diamondtrade.stm.

3. Economy Is More, Much More than the Monetary

From visions for the world let us go back to the fulfillment of our needs of livelihood—the core business of economics. Needs of livelihood are being fulfilled by the manifold activities of a host of actors, a large part of whom does not operate through monetized markets, and this is also true in highly monetized societies.[1] In other words, in order to get what we need we do not always go to a shop and spend money. Mothers and fathers cook, care, and clean. Children help their parents. Friends, neighbours, and relatives render services to each other, not to mention the institutionalised voluntary work in communities. All non-paid activities that keep us fed, healthy, and that educate us are productive processes that serve our urgent needs of livelihood. But they are never counted in any economic survey. "Not counted is not valued" is the standpoint of most policymakers. But take these non-monetary services away, and the economy will crumble, including the monetary part of it.[2]

Whether a society treasures a culture of rendering free services to one another or whether this is seen as a waste of time depends on the values that are alive in that society. From the point of view of true macroeconomic thinking, however, any activity that fulfills the needs of beings is productive activity and therefore deserves attention. A community where the goodwill to give each other the diverse necessities of life for free abundantly exists has thereby uncovered a source

---

1. A comparative study across 13 industrial countries suggests that slightly less than half (49%) of the total work time is spent in paid SNA (Systems of National Accounts) activities and slightly more than half (51%) in unpaid non-SNA activities. (Source: United Nations Development Programme (UNDP), Human Development Report (HDR), 1995, Chapter 4, pp. 93–94).
2. Rough estimates show that $16 trillion (or 70%) of the $23 trillion of global output is performed in the non-monetary sector. This estimate includes the value of unpaid work by men and women as well as the underpayment of women's work in the market. Of this $16 trillion, $11 trillion is the non-monetized contribution of women. (Source: UNDP, HDR 1995, Chapter 4, p.97).

of wealth. We do not speak of aspects like personal satisfaction and wholesome relatedness. This book is not about such moral values. We speak of obtaining the goods and services that we need to live. The existence of a joyful will to assist each other in this way is an economic good. Macroeconomic policymakers should take a clear view of this fact. To exclude the non-monetized productive sector from their planning is a mistake they cannot afford to make, and society will have to pay.

Free services can go around in the private sphere or in the communal sphere. They can come from governmental structures or from business initiatives. Free services can be rendered in the fields of food, health, sports, education, or in any other aspect of livelihood. Not only do they satisfy individual needs that otherwise might go unfulfilled, but in doing so, they very likely avoid societal damage and costs. In poor economies such damages and costs add up to the already existing hindrances to development and so hamper the monetized sector of the economy as well. In welfare states such damages and costs will eventually show up on the money side of the economy, because state budgets must pay for policies that repair. Therefore, policymakers who plan for development and policymakers who must guard balanced budgets may do well to uncover the wealth of the non-monetized productive sector. Too much focus on growing Gross National Product figures alone may take away our sight on increasing costs and less fulfillment of needs, which happens while we grow.

When speaking of the benefits of such voluntary activity, we do stress, however, that they must be done in liberty. When unpaid activity becomes a part of an economy that is exploitative then it becomes a part of poverty, and policies must seek to increase people's productivity and needs fulfillment by supporting them with additional strength. But when the provision of free service is a matter of voluntary interest of people, then policies can further enhance and stimulate such unpaid work, whether it be in the home or in the community. In that case policies are just a matter of creating good conditions but never of compulsory patterns.

Diverse economies and cultures may value unpaid work differently. Gratitude for household work done well, the honour of helping one another, the obligation of private profit to benefit the common good may be rated high or low. But in general we can say that a society that does not know such liberty is poor, however large its rate of economic growth may be.

We come back to this unpaid work that is more of a compulsion of poverty than a free source of wealth. We want to take a moment to look at it in relation to growing economies and successful industrialisation. We have already seen that the micro-logic of individuals, businesses, and states will by default lead to the exploitation of others, and "these others" are by default people with less strength. Rich nations exploit the people of poor nations, for instance, by a mechanism we call "comparative advantage." It is a neutral term when used between partners of equal strength but a euphemism for exploitation—of cheap labour or resources—when applied between economies at unequal levels of development.

In rapidly developing nations, for instance the Asian tigers[3], the capitalised classes build their earning power on the exploitative labour of marginalised compatriots. And also in nations that are neither developed nor rapidly developing there always exists a well-to-do elite. Whether their privileges are founded on a class of deprived people who work but do not earn is something for them to see or to deny.

I do not feel it is necessary to name cases and tell stories. Too many reports, investigations, and studies have already done just that. They show us the relation between profits for some and unpaid or underpaid work by others. And the others are always people with less strength. Sometimes they are ethnic minorities, or immigrants, or women, or children; it really does not matter, they are all people. Sometimes they work in overcrowded cities, in rural areas, in free export zones, in subcontractors' sweatshops, or in private homes of others or their own; it really does not matter, the work is exploitative. This kind of non-monetized or underpaid work also needs policy: not one that sustains the work, but one that sustains the people.

And then there is that other kind of non-monetary economy. Not so much one of free services, but one of barter and exchange without the intermediary of money. Exchange is done by practical value against practical value, or distribution occurs by way of well-defined social relationships. Millions of people in this world survive in this way day after day. Are such economies underdeveloped, poor, and backward? Can they be ignored and wiped out by the interests of a money economy? As long as the members of that community can maintain their basic livelihood and have control over their lives, these are vibrant economies and dignified people. In the name of "progress" and "development," however, more complex economies have destroyed the livelihoods of many who survived by sub-

---

3. "Asian Tigers" refer to the economies of Taiwan, Hongkong, South Korea, and Singapore; these nations were noted for maintaining high growth rates and rapid industrialisation between the early 1960s and 1990s.

sistence economies and barter. The invariable consequence is not only damaged livelihoods, but also mental and spiritual disarray for people who lost their way of life that was their self-empowered strategy to live and to survive.

These are not only stories of a colonial past, but very much of today. Logging of timber forests and mining of gold and copper are just some random contemporary examples.[4] Capital-heavy industries come in and exploit resources for money profits that always leave the country. What stays behind are destroyed habitats and disturbed livelihoods of people whose protests sound long and loud. But growth policies, so we have heard, just don't have good ears. Interdependent economy wants to take a hard look at such monetized policies of poverty and commands instead not to make money but to nurture life—for that is the true purpose of economic policy.

---

4.   See Appendix B on "Mining in the South."

4. Full Employment—Does It Command Economic Growth?

A macroeconomic planner, when he cares for people, will seek to increase employment opportunities. Nobody can reason that logic away, and interdependent economy does not intend to do that. However, this first logic leads to a second that goes "employment opportunities come with growing economies." But here things are not as simple as they appear. The reality we experience is compelling: more business immediately creates more jobs. If that reality were also long-term, then by now countries that have known good growth rates over the past decades and centuries would have far outgrown unemployment. Unemployment would have become outdated, a condition we can hardly remember, something of an obscure past. But alas, the truth is that unemployment is here to stay, because, in fact, it is linked to growth. And in particular it is linked to growth of the monetary kind. The higher a society rates the monetary side of its economy, the more we see the appearance of unemployment. How does that happen?

Picture for instance a society where livelihood is organised around the production for basic and direct demand, and money markets play a minor role or no role at all. We may think of societies that sustain themselves by hunting, small husbandry, or basic agriculture. Or we may even remind ourselves of city economies like those in medieval Europe. Here manufacturers produce their artefacts on demand from clients known to them rather than for anonymous markets. Are such societies plagued by massive unemployment? No, all productive labour is regularly employed in producing what society demands. Safe for natural catastrophes, the outbreak of epidemics, or warfare, these are stable societies where the economy harmoniously turns around and around. And it is true, it turns without much growth potential. To go one step lower still—a troupe of animals will be occupied from morning till evening with either happy play or the acquisition of its means of subsistence. Unemployment is something unknown to them and, it is true, neither is increase in quality of life.

It is developed economies that manifest this new phenomenon of massive unemployment. And why is that? It is because the richness is derived from efficient production processes that decrease the need for human labour, from heavily capitalised production and giant corporations, which rise and fall make great waves. It is derived from high mobility and global interconnectedness that leave us with less control. It comes with constant change and innovation, which is equal to discontinuity. And it requires massive marketing of products that we do not immediately require or sometimes do not require at all. Sales of these products will quickly drop when empty expectations at stock exchange markets and other speculative gains collapse. These are the marked aspects of economies bent on growth, but also aspects of massive, but unstable markets, and thus of mass employment that comes and goes.

The purpose here is not to romanticise simple societies and demonise dynamic economies; it is just to put things into perspective. If we choose to have a growth economy we have to reckon with unemployment as a matter of fact. Unemployment is a cost factor that must be accounted for all along and not surprise us now and then. How economic policy must account for it, and who must be accountable is a question for further investigation. At this point interdependent economy just wants to wake us up from the dream that more growth will overcome unemployment.

The unemployment discussed above must be distinguished, however, from the structural lack of basic economic activity in a society. The fate of people who must live with insufficient structure to sustain livelihood is a different one. Here different analysis and different measures must bring solutions. Societies that seek development of basic structure must start from within and from the beginning. Inherent productive forces of land and people, with full ownership of the process by the people of the land, must be built step by step. Development is an issue in itself and we will address it at a later point.

So I have argued that unemployment is linked with economies that grow, and simply accounting for it all along is the only real policy. Indeed, that is the immediate response to this occurrence of instability. But let us probe into the matter a little further. What we see is an inherent contradiction in the policy approach to growth and unemployment. I quote a recent policy paper of the Netherlands Ministry of Economic Affairs, which is no doubt representative, or should I say symptomatic, of all state policies pursuing growth.

The Dutch government is presently (2003) confronted with falling growth rates and rising unemployment figures. The policy paper,[1] as expected, displays the rhetoric of a "necessary increase of labour participation and growth of productivity." But what are these strategies for growth of productivity? These are innovation, dynamism, enhanced competitiveness, and efficiency. There is no doubt that when all these good visions for industrial revival materialise there will be economic growth, but in the process people must lose jobs. Innovation means old trades must go, new technology means present knowledge becomes obsolete, and more efficiency means less need of employees.

I want to point out still another set of words in this same policy paper that I find difficult to rhyme: "The European Union has set itself the goal…an economy that can produce sustainable growth, with more and better jobs and *closer-knit social cohesion.*" (italics added) Innovation has indeed proven that in time it can produce growth and new jobs, albeit it has not proven that everybody can maintain a job in an economic environment of ever-changing technology. But the positive relation between more work and more social cohesion is one of serious doubt. However, the topic here was unemployment, and let's go back to this. From all these policy controversies and with these good social values nevertheless in the back of my mind, I conclude that a drastically different approach to the issue of employment may be due.

Unemployment may, in the end, not be so much a product of growth, as I myself argued, but of an obsolete concept of employment. Where economic development is low and existing productivity can barely keep us all alive, full employment of each and every individual makes economic sense. But where innovation and technology have taken up the job of working for our needs, it almost is as if the system itself demands a new approach. That is to bring down the use of manpower in the economy. Not to honour this demand is having to experience the protest of the system: the arising of massive unemployment from time to time.

Why indeed continue to work full force in the drudgery of seeking livelihood when the job is already done? Trying to find good answers to this question may, I suspect, also help in our quest for better social cohesion. Whereas to link this human value with the growth of employment is an error our politicians should not make.

---

1.   Ministry of Economic Affairs of the Netherlands, *"Memorie van Toelichting Begroting Economische Zaken 2004,"* 16 September 2003. (Explanatory Memorandum on the Budget of Economic Affairs 2004).

5. Money, Prices, and Value—Theory or Productivity?

It is the dream of all economic planners to be able to predict cleared markets, to compute the right prices, and to understand value. Micro-and macro-economists alike would love to be able to fix the perfect price at which markets will balance, to determine the right money volume at which producers will produce and consumers will consume in perfect harmony and ensure full employment at the same time.

One theory says: free market and free competition will, as by an invisible hand, fix the perfect price at which markets are fully cleared and needs are efficiently fulfilled. The other theory says: centralised planning will pay each worker what his productive labour is worth and provide him with all his needs. And in between these two extreme models of economy we have modelled mathematical formula to predict the outcome of our money and price policies. The problem with these perfect theories is that their instances in reality never exist. Time lapses, information lapses, and "irrational" economic human behaviour create an environment in which prices and volumes are never the logical outcome of a mathematical calculation.

Do balanced markets have a price? Or in other words, can we calculate stability and buy the perfect economy? If that were so, life would be easy. We would print our economies at our national banks and compute our markets with our formula. In reality however, whatever we try to compute or plan, products keep appearing at the wrong time, at the wrong place, in the wrong quantity, at the wrong price. Overheated economies, inflation, recession, budgetary deficits, trade imbalances, non-matching labour markets…the reality often is a nightmare for economic planners. But what is worse, the reality often is a nightmare for millions of people. Whatever goods may be available at the market and foodstuffs are stored in granaries, whatever money volumes may speed around this globe—the basic needs of many are never fulfilled.

In real life what counts for real people is not efficient markets or equilibrium prices. What really counts is the relativity between the prices on the market and the money in our pockets, in other words: our purchasing power. And again here, in the end it is fulfilling our needs of livelihood that really counts. As long as we can buy what we need, life is fine. For many life is fine today at price levels five to ten times higher than thirty or forty years ago, as it was fine then. For many others in this world life is not fine and has not been for a very long time; they do not have the purchasing power to buy life's necessities, and they do not have the productive strength to make what they need.

As we design our policies on money and prices—including the price of money and the price of labour—we should know that money must be other-powered. Money in itself is powerless and its policies do not touch the deeper causes of stable markets and growth potential. It is the *inherent productivity*[1] of people put to use in sustainable modes of production that lends its value to the money. Such productivity of people makes the difference between affluence and want. Good health and able skills are basic aspects of people's productivity. And so we are back where we began—fulfilling the needs of livelihood. Depending on the actual circumstances of people, the state of their economy, their priorities, and their choices, increasing productivity may come with different policy emphases. It may be sending girls to school or adults to computer courses. It may be giving people basic health care or introducing new and holistic systems of cure and prevention. It may be the set up of co-operations or the individualisation of work to the home. It may be the use of simple agricultural methodologies or the introduction of high-tech. It may be making governments more lean and clean or providing state services of quality performance. The list is endless but the focus is one: improve the inherent productivity of people in both the monetary and the non-monetary sector of the economy, support their health and train their skills.

If we employ money policies to regulate consumption and production in tune with policies that improve on the qualitative structures for people—so they can live, produce, and consume at least at basic levels—then there is less risk of overheating and prices will remain affordable. If money is pumped into an economy—from abroad or by national banks—without simultaneously taking care of people's productivity, then hyperinflation will make people poor, and that will not give us stable economies. If restrictive policies make money scarce and

---

1.   Inherent productivity is the term we introduce here to denote that kind of productivity by which an individual can make a positive contribution to society while at the same time asserting his own being. It is this concept that guards against the danger of productive work becoming exploitative work.

thereby squeeze livelihoods that are already at bottom line, then this is poverty caused by common will and not by individual misfortune.

Mathematical formulae computing balanced growth can never capture all the variables that exist in the world. But policies directed at keeping all people involved in the economic cycle of production and consumption at modes of sustainable quality, while keeping a view of both the monetary and non-monetary side of the economy, will guarantee the stability needed for further growth. Why is that? Because "to spread risk is to minimise risk" as a well-known adage in matters of financial management says. Spreading the economy over all participants, therefore, is to minimise the risk of disequilibrium to the maximum. Keeping all of us involved in the economy does not lead to stability; it *is* stability. An economy that upholds the basic purchasing power of all upholds the basic demand for much. Ongoing demand upholds ongoing production. In this way such policies that spread the risk—instead of leaving many people at risk—ensures an ongoing cycle of economic activity. Without wanting to make any predictions, interdependent economy declares that this is the best we can do for stable markets and affordable prices, nationally and globally.

At the same time, to support and maintain people's inherent productivity constitutes a cost factor of production and therefore is a part of price. The consumer, as a micro-unit, naturally sees ever-lower prices as his economic interest. But when macro-policies (planning for "industry's competitiveness") favour structures of ever-lower costs, then we must also ask the question: who will pay the price of upholding sustainability? Macro-economic planners should know that low prices are not always the best buy. Economic policy should organise cycles of production and consumption that sustain life. This simply is the price we must pay for maintaining our purchasing power.

6. State Budgets and Commerce—One Interest, One Logic

It seems to be a fact of life: states and their governors identify strongly with the interests of commerce and industry. This means that these "motors of the economy" are the natural partners of states. States and their governors have two tasks: to make laws and regulations, and to take up activities that as a society we decide are the task of the state. To implement these tasks states need to collect money; whether this money serves to keep up armies or to fund social schemes, states need money to fulfill their governing tasks. Therefore, their outlook is naturally focused on micro-agents in society that are at the source of money-generation, and it is hard for states to direct their priorities to the broader aim of fulfilling the collective economic needs of citizens, that is, to sustain the inherent productivity of people.

In its final analysis, after much political strife and struggle, it is the state's budget that determines the state's programme. This justified responsibility of states to balance budgets, however, has become tightly bound to the economics of growth. We need more money, so we pursue growth of money income and this again is equated with economic growth. This logic stands and is never questioned. Does anyone ever ask if economic growth leads to more state expenditure therefore causing policies to become like snakes biting their own tails? Or does anyone ever investigate whether less growth but better needs fulfillment could lead to a decrease in state expenditure? Interdependent economy says: the requirement to balance budgets does not mean that state and economic growth must be tied up in this sacred bond. Policies aimed at this broad-based inherent productivity of people, together with conscientious management of state funds are the efficiency rationale for budgets that must balance.

See how far out of balance the belief in growth got us, how high on the scale of insanity. Any politician or economic advisor can cry out without risk to his reputation the appeal that consumers should consume more in order to stimulate the economy. But is this notion not in fact the ultimate defeat of mankind? Human needs are made subordinate to something abstract as the economy. This appeal tells us that the economy is not there to serve our needs; no, we must buy in order to serve the economy. Two realities are possible when a consumer is not buying: either he already has what he needs and he does not need to buy anymore, or he does not have what he needs but does not have the money to buy. To make the appeal to non-buyers that they should buy is to either sell them things they do not need—and this is bad economy—or to convince people that they should go into debt in order to buy—and this is bad counselling.

Present policies relegate awareness about our real needs to the dark regions of our psyche, individual and collective. The needs of the growth economy, in contrast, are placed in the full light of day. For centuries mankind has struggled to free himself from systems and dictators, only to surrender himself to the dictate of a system—the system of the growth economy.

History of states was always closely linked with the fate of their elites, formerly knights in armour and later captains of industry. But now we have reached the moment in time that the stature of the state is with the power of its people, or so we say. For economic policies this implies that growth has become a concept of the past. Instead it must be people's economic participation and the quality of it that must take central stage. It is again confusing the individual's concern with that of the macroeconomic task. The individual producers and consumers as by instinct will take care of pursuing growth. State's macro-policies, therefore, can be discharged.

Power and invincibility are the natural goals of states. Maintaining law and order and generating money income are strategies already known. But now, keeping all citizens within the economic cycle while not depriving other nations of that same good is a new rationale that in this interdependent world no one can defeat.

7. Our Real Needs—Who Defines?

We have been talking much about the needs of people and that effective macro-economic measures should aim at fulfilling these. Now the question arises: who decides what our real needs are? There exists no higher agent who decides on that, nor do we intend to fix one. It can only be the dynamics of all parties in a society that comes with choices and decides on priorities. It is a dynamism that can never be perfect, will never bring definite solutions, is in constant flux, and comes in different appearances in different cultures.

Awareness is the key word. The more awareness exists with the people involved—self-awareness of their own true needs and awareness of the interrelatedness of life—the more successful the dynamism will fulfill its task. The key word is not democracy, at least not in the sense of multiparty, parliamentary governing. A highly hierarchic culture where dependent people look up to the patriarch to take care of them may very well provide for their needs and let them live in dignity at the same time. It all depends on this awareness. In this book about economics we do not deal further with this human quality, how to increase it and whether there is good and bad in it. These are matters for other disciplines like education and personal development. However, the approach of interdependent economy warrants the best possible result to be obtained in any given situation…and it gives us the awareness that awareness is important.

Now I mentioned culture and its link with people's needs. And we may already understand that different cultures value different needs. But what defines, in the context of the economy, the term culture? Literature, artistic expression, song and dance, dress and cuisine may be considered as cultural. But these are not the core issues when dealing with production, distribution, and consumption. The culture that counts for the economy and in fact is quite inseparable with it is the inner sense of individuals about their interrelatedness with one another and with their natural habitat. The inner-felt values that rule these relationships in a particular group of people are the basic fabric of life for these people, and that is their culture. Whether these inner-felt values are good or bad is not the issue here. What is the issue here is that these values define the culture of a people, and that this is the pattern that organises their economy best.

To illustrate this we can look at two opposing examples. A culture of individuality, where interrelatedness and mutual responsibility have faded to a thin line, will organise its economy around independence and high mobility. A culture where the sense of bonding between the members of a group is so strong as to forbid any thought of someone pursuing his individual career will organise its economy around group activity and loyalty. A culture by which nature is an object of science will analyse its potential and exploit it like dead matter. A culture that knows nature to be part of one whole life system will interact with it in order to sustain life.

Let us have a little interlude with an example not of my invention. Here below I print a text by Mohammad Hatta, Muslim and vice president of Indonesia under President Sukarno from 1945 to 1956. The excerpt is from a speech held at Aligarh University, India, on October 29, 1955.[1]

> *One means of achieving social justice is through the cooperative movement which gives rise to joint endeavours on a basis of mutual help. Cooperative organisations are truly in keeping with the ideals of Islam because Islam places upon the individual the responsibility for the well being of the entire community. Further, in order to secure social security in accordance with Islam, the state should represent a welfare state, which guarantees the prosperity of all. And not only material prosperity, but also, chiefly, spiritual wealth.*

Looking at the reality of Indonesia today we wonder what it is that has hindered the country with a population that is almost 90% Muslim to establish an economy in accordance with its own culture. It is not the lack of high development that we question here, but can we speak of a welfare state when there is not even a hint of free access to basic health care for the poorest? Now this of course is an exercise meant for policymakers of all countries and all cultures. What are their people's values of human interrelatedness and its bond with nature? And is the way in which their economy produces, distributes, and consumes in concord with that? And for economies of global reach, this question must be answered for their international policies as well. A perfect match is not what we expect, but at least we hope not to compare day and night. And certainly, we do not mean to fix rigidity. Cultural value systems were never meant to stay where they are; they are

---

1. Mohammad Hatta, Portrait of a Patriot, selected writings by Mohammad Hatta, The Hague, Paris, 1972, p. 602.

multi-faceted in themselves, and what is more, culture determines the economy and economy moves the culture.

In international relations, too often, we have judged the one culture against the other and have found it necessary to intervene. Intervention, sometimes out of sheer greed, sometimes out of noble intentions, can tear apart the basic fabric of life—economically and culturally—of those that undergo the intervention. These are not only stories of the past, but very much of today.

In international relations, therefore, what interdependent economy proposes is not necessarily to condemn all intervention, but for the intervening agent to take a few steps back...to take many steps back, to stay so far back that cultures can start to see themselves, instead of always looking up to an outside example. Cultures that seek development should then start to practice awareness, self-awareness of their own inner-felt values, and then organise their economies around their own people. Hopefully, agents of macroeconomic policy will plan for the fulfillment of needs of people first and then derive sub-goals—maybe growth and trade or maybe subsistence production and home-grown manufacturing. Hopefully, people will increase their self-awareness and know what their real needs are. Hopefully, the top and the bottom will interact and give each other checks and balances. On the basis of such cultural self-awareness true demands for intervention from outside can be formulated, and a dignified exchange between two cultures can take place.

Good international economic relations start with the self-awareness of those who seek development. Economy, culture, and people's sense of life's values are only different faces of one life experience. Destroy any one of these faces and this society will be disfigured and become impotent as to its own development. One wonders if maybe, just maybe, such economic impotence is what occurs in the over-developed economies of today? Could it be that in some rich societies the economic law of diminishing marginal utility is at work? In other words, do they keep producing and consuming more and more, while additional satisfaction becomes less and less? If so, then these economies are becoming less and less efficient. While seeking more growth they are going along a downward curve on the scale of needs fulfilling. If so, a further focus on quantity of production and consumption will only blur the view on the quality of how they live. A people's culture, its life values about interrelatedness, is expressed in the economy—both quantity *and quality*. Both must be rich for people to feel satisfied. So maybe we should say that good international relations start with the self-awareness of those who seek more development and the self-awareness of those who seek more satisfaction.

Interdependent economy sees economy and culture as interlinked. A people that is not happy at how it works and consumes must seek to re-evaluate life's human values and express these in their economy. A people that seeks development from material poverty must found it on the happiness its culture brings. Treasuring the values of one's own culture while leaving the culture of others intact is the basic platform on which economic international relations must take place—for human plurality is the real richness of our world.

8. Culture and Economic Resources

So we have seen that people's awareness of their own needs and own value systems will determine their own economy. Awareness alone, however, will not do of course. To sustain livelihood we need some hardware too. A people of one cultural identity with one particular way of life that treasures its distinct set of values must *own its economic resources.* If cultural distinction exists at sub-national levels then so should ownership of resources also be distinct. Let us name some of these resources: land, water, raw materials, sources of energy, natural habitat, knowledge, and skills. Further they can be the institutionalising of finance, the legal system, the educational system, communication infrastructure, media, and still other vital aspects of life in society. For it is this ownership that empowers a people to think, plan, and act according to its own way of life. Present policies, international and national, too often reduce weaker economies to mere events in the greater plans of others. These plans of others make use of the resources according to the plans of others.

A people that wants to further an economy of its own must avail of its own resources. This is the hard-core basis for inherent economic development. To speak of international cooperation without inherent ownership of resources is beguilement. To speak of national development without safeguarding one's ownership of resources is self-deception. Interdependent economy wants to sustain people's livelihoods. But when we speak of fulfilling the necessities of life we do not mean a life of mere vegetation and consumption. We mean a life in dignity and of rich humanity.

Wherever good quality of life now flourishes, it occurred through ownership of resources. Not one of these rich economies was helped to its development by the design of strangers with a different lifestyle importing a foreign system. It was by the investment of own resourcefulness that inherent development could take place; and furthermore it was by the protection of own productivity that infant industries could mature. May true international cooperation of today replace the colonial exploitation of the past—may that be one lesson learned. May development cooperation take place in the context of a people's own culture and set of values—may that be a second lesson learned. International cooperation that develops dependency on foreign trade and foreign capital is mere continuation of global exploitation and local poverty—may that be an observation that we are willing to learn from now.

Much has been written and said about the imperialistic economic policies of the industrialised countries. People's protest against it goes from civil society activity at civilised international forums, over unsettling demonstrations at meetings of world powers, to brutal acts of terrorism on any territory in the world. Decades of dialogue at endless international forums will not save a people. Acts of terrorism will only destroy people. Dialogue can be constructive, and destructive acts can be forgiven. But in the end people must—if they want to be effective—speak up there where the immediate responsibility lies: at their own national governments and their own national institutions. If imperialistic policies harm the people of a weaker nation, it is the latter's government that allows this to happen. When nations go about their imperialistic policies it is their "democratic" people that allows them to do so. It no doubt needs courage and sacrifice to stand up and demand from one's elites a change of policies. And in some nations it needs more than in others. But this is exactly what brings about well-governed nations. Good governance never came as a gift from heaven. It must come as a result of long-time effort by masses of men and women, some of whom must take the lead and forge new visions. Sometimes this is a doom scenario of suppressed opposition and human rights abuse, and true, this book has no solution for such outrageous pains. What interdependent economy does, however, is to provide us with the weapon of reason and hope that the understanding of its principles—nationally and internationally, by the people and their governors—will lessen the pressures and shorten the struggle.

9. Informal Economy—Ignored Economy

From politics let us return to economics. In all economies there exists an area of so-called informal economy. One could also call it the invisible economy, because it is not registered and therefore it is not accounted for in any Gross National Product figures. Invisible in numbers it becomes ignored by policy. Ignored is its importance for the survival of millions of people from day to day. Ignored is its potential for future development. Especially in those economies that we call developing, the informal economy plays a major role.[1] If planners and policy-makers would turn their attention to this sector they would probably find a wealth of growth potential. Rather than straining at cramped attempts to trade with uneven partners in faraway countries under forbidding regulations, one would do better to sustain, support, and improve the economic vibrancy of one's informal sector. Surely, some individuals in the informal sector are doing fine and have no need for intervention from above. The large majority, however, struggles with lack of property rights, lack of capital, lack of infrastructure, lack of just about anything except insecurity. If workers are lucky they can maintain this small base to the end of their days. If they are less lucky they may even lose this little existence and drop out of the informal economy to the realm of no economy at all.

Much research has already been done on the facts and needs of the informal sector. A pile of literature and papers informs those who care to know. But knowing the informal sector is one thing; making it a policy priority is another. Let global thinking not distract local attention from what is near and prime—let true logic prevail. Where people's initiative is already at work, it is mere common sense to see that with relatively little effort this can be turned into higher gears of development. Instead, planners choose to neglect the small but many and select the bigger favours of a few. Alas, planners choose to neglect this original potential and prefer to import imitations. Let planners take good reconnaissance of this

---

1. See Appendix C on "The Informal Sector."

ignored sector, and, no doubt, the sensible policies will reveal themselves to their vision.

10. Where Is the Freedom in Free Trade?

Trade, in the mind of most people, is naturally linked with the notion of wealth creation and improved fulfillment of needs—the trading creates profit, and one can obtain goods that oneself does not produce. So, wherever trade arises by natural inclination of man that is fine and it needs no further scrutinising. It is the micro-logic of the individual at work, and thanks to that instinct we live.

In the mind also of macroeconomic planners and policymakers trade creates economic growth. But planners and policymakers should know that it is not the trade as such that makes the growth. When between two individuals the one happens to have cows and the other happens to have grain, and they decide to exchange some of it, then their needs are better fulfilled and, therefore, the transaction is fine. But total wealth in society has not increased.

Adam Smith, indeed, in his analyses enlightened us about the fact that it is the *division of labour* that increases wealth, and from division of labour, naturally, comes trade. The specialisation on the production of one article and then trading it, instead of trying to produce everything one needs oneself, increases the efficiency of that production process. In this way total wealth of society increases. And we were enlightened even further by David Ricardo who explained to us the *law of comparative advantage*, propounding that total wealth would increase if each country focuses on doing what it does best.[1] Thus by maximising total production, countries will trade their surplus production with each other. In this way both theories point out to us the origins of growth: not trade itself, but specialised production increases overall efficiency and quantity.

Planners and policymakers, however, should not only be well informed about the theory behind the slogan "trade is good for growth," they are called to think much deeper still. For fulfilling people's needs is the real aim of macroeconomic

---

1.   David Ricardo (1772–1823) was a British economist. His law of comparative advantage is often not well understood. It only applies in an international environment where capital and labour is *not* mobile. Nevertheless, rightly or wrongly, the theory is often brought forward by proponents of free trade in today's globalised economy.

policy; whereas growth can only be the means to an end. This true aim of macro-economic policy is well implied, and maybe unintentionally so, in Smith's and Ricardo's theories for growth. Division of labour and comparative advantage both say that people must produce before they trade. It is indeed the opportunity to produce that provides people with what they need. And furthermore, it is the need to *continue* to produce that leads us to require that producers have a stable market share.

And here we have arrived at the heart of all policies on trade. Trade itself, as we have seen, is an activity that comes quite naturally; the individual will pursue trade almost as a matter of instinct. What does not come so naturally and in contrast requires long and hard battle is the market share, or in other words the outlet opportunity for the productive activity. Why do policies on free trade always need to be so contentious if trade simply is the motor for growth, a desire on which we all agree? Because free trade policies are not for liberty, but to obtain, protect, and expand a nation's market share. The arsenal on this battlefield is complex and construed: tariffs, quotas, quantitative restrictions, quality requirements, boxes in different colours,[2] preferential treatment, special products, special safeguards, and still more. This avalanche of rules and regulations shows that trade is everything but free, and that is exactly how nations intend it to be.

Having discovered what the real issue is, let us now turn our attention to the actual object of contention: the market share. People are dependent on markets as outlets for their productivity so they can earn their own way. The simple conclusion, therefore, is that a well-devised system of market share distribution is the policy that people need. Certain markets—for commodities, manufactured goods or services—that are basic for a nation's economic life should be organised and distributed bearing in mind people's needs for consumption and production. Starting from total demand, that is world market volume, we can then go on to allocate to each nation market shares that make economic sense and at prices that are right. To *organise* and *distribute* market shares implies that we do not need to enter into battle and thus can do away with tariffs, coloured boxes, and so on. Basic quantities of truly Organised World Trade (OWT) must provide developing nations and their people with the opportunity to earn a basic living. Concern-

---

2. The World Trade Organisation (WTO) has devised boxes in three colours: amber, green, and blue. Each contains a group of protectionist measures applied by national policies. The colour designates the degree of their "trade-distorting" effect and thereby WTO policy for their more or less urgent elimination.

ing sectors and volumes of trade that are for further growth above basic levels, nations can measure up their strength and continue to be contentious over complex restrictive instruments.

Such a system of OWT is primarily meant to hedge developing economies. But as an advantageous side effect, it will also regulate the economy of the developed world. Whereas in the past want was the problem, today we have an overkill. Technical advancement increased our productive power to levels now largely exceeding our consumptive needs, that is, on world scale. Milk, meat, coffee, cotton, sugar, maize, rice, and wheat are just some examples of commodities that would drown us if each producer would produce the volumes he technically can do. Fortunately, we have the restricting mechanism of the market, but the restrictions must be shared. To allot protected market shares to some will automatically contain overproduction by others.[3]

Overproduction and people's poverty, existing side by side, are two strong arguments for a system of organised world trade or OWT. Can someone please explain the arguments for the free trade policies of the WTO that do not make people free?

---

3.   Oxfam published two papers on subsidy of cotton (USA) and sugar (EU) production. See Bibliography.

11. Accumulation of Capital and Quality of Life

The other myth that has outgrown its own meaning is the good of accumulation of financial capital.[1] Again here, the individual entrepreneur or shareholder's company gathers capital to start business and seeks to increase capital in order to enlarge business. The individual consumer saves money for future security as a matter of instinct. The more the better and the micro-logic is clear. Also for society, capital and the growth of it have proved to be a blessing. The development and application of technology that makes our lives more comfortable, mass production that makes goods more affordable, infrastructure and institutions that serve the common good, and the increase of productivity that enriches us with time for services and leisure that were formerly unknown are all accomplishments of productive power saved up, so bigger heaps could finance greater things. There is no doubt that capital accumulation has improved our quality of life, and it still holds promise for the future.

But now there is a question that we should ask. Is it the ever-growing concentration of capital by itself that will continue to create these wonders, or must we *guard* the quality of capital and more particularly of what it does? And once again, interdependent economy answers that fulfilling the needs of beings must be the aim and not mere growth.

Let us take a closer look into the specifics of this force of capital. The inherent nature of capital is such that it must be invested and be profitable; capital is always working capital. Capital can never sit still and do nothing like the money that we carry in our pockets. So what happens when the capital that one owner owns grows and grows. Can he still maintain a view on the real value of investments, whether it is good or bad? No, these heaps of capital must wander off to distant profit opportunities where his eyes cannot distinguish quality and where

---

1. There are other forms of capital—equally important for the economy—like human skill, knowledge, natural resources, or technology, but these are not being discussed here.

only figures count. The owner has no knowledge of the concrete forces his capital unleashes, nor does he care to know. Working capital becomes capital "without interest" in the environment of people and societies that host its need to work. Or worse, disinterested capital may dictate its own environment on people and societies. And this is an environment conducive to the undisturbed growth of capital, taking disturbance of people's lives as the easy price to pay.[2]

And then there is a further practice of making capital work. Disinterested capital can still be meant to be productive, to create goods of value. But speculative capital merely comes and goes by the volatility of figures in their abstraction and thus makes profit by producing absolutely nothing.[3] The micro-unit—person or institution—knows only one effect: the increase of monetary units he can call his own. The macro-world knows another effect: more money volume against less real value, and that is rising prices or inflation. Prices that become so inflated they blow up in our face and values plummet down to worthlessness,[4] just like a balloon inflated with too much air will give a big bang leaving nothing behind.

Trade for price differences alone—in companies' shares, foreign currency, crude oil, or wheat—is trade in empty value. Heaps of accumulated capital desperately seeking to work have created jobs for themselves like the financial derivatives that trade in numbers only. Originally designed to hedge against insecurity of real business investments and thus creating the economic good of security, they are now also massively used for no hedging need at all. Futures, options, and certificates of stock exchange indices are trade in expectation of the rise and fall of numbers, sometimes being combined averages of a list of other numbers. Investment in these derivatives for mere volatility of numbers is not much different from turning the wheel at the roulette table. Gains are made; nothing is produced. And not only is there the simple rate of profit on the capital, but there also

---

2.   Worldwide popular protest against plans to establish a Multilateral Agreement on Investment (MAI) shows the opposing interests of human livelihood and global free traffic of investments that are conducive to further concentration of capital accumulation there where it already abundantly exists. The negotiations took place at the OECD platform (1997) but were halted.

3.   International currency transactions total more than U.S. $1 trillion a day, more than 80% of this trading is of a speculative nature. In comparison: U.S. $220 billion a day is the world's production of goods and services.

4.   The world has recently known a number of international financial crises due to fast movement of massive amounts of capital between currencies: Mexico (1994), Southeast Asia (1997), Russia (1998), Brazil (1999), and Argentina (2001). As a consequence of these crises millions of people in developing countries have lost jobs and were pushed into poverty and debt. (Source: www.waronwant.org).

is a multiplying factor at work. Trade in these derived numbers requires only a fraction of the value of the underlying capital while the profits are the same (for instance the price of options on shares of a company is a fraction of the value of the underlying shares). Add to this that investment "without capital," that is with borrowed money, is another new banking product offered to those with sufficient collateral, then the leverage effect of "capital creating more capital" clearly can be seen to be enormous.

One wonders what added quality of life for people can be created by cycle after cycle of profits made on numbers only. One also wonders what the effect is of concentration of capital in the hands of some few instead of capital formation that is evenly spread. I do not bemoan the fact of some possessing more than others. Interdependent economy does not see a fundamental fault in that. I do, however, fear the destabilising effect of heavy capitalisation here and lack of capital there on markets everywhere—be they for money or for food. And most of all I fear the destabilising effect on people's basic livelihoods.

To make capital available for productive investment is the real function of the world of finance. See how far the lead of growth made banks stray from their original purpose. Aimlessness of capital cannot be the goal of macro-policies. Instead, increase of quality of life for all is the mandate for governors that oversee finance. It is the duty of citizens to demand policies that give us just that, and, in the interdependent world of today, to give all of us just that.

Speculative money that speeds around the globe has already been disqualified by many, and some support the concept of the Tobin Tax.[5] I do not intend to make concrete policy designs here or discuss proposed policies in-depth, as I do not underestimate the complexity of international policies on money. However, the Tobin Tax comes with globally institutionalised solutions. Interdependent economy does not favour further global institutionalising, at least not until assertive national policy-making has materialised. National governments are still the ones from whom people can demand direct accountability. True, governments are often imperfect, and, indeed, accountability is rarely delivered. But can bad national governance be overruled by global institutions? To bring policing to global levels will place control even more out of reach of people. That holds true for

---

5.   The Tobin Tax is named after the economist and Nobel laureate (1981) James Tobin. He proposed a system of Currency Transaction Tax in the 1970s. The rationale was that a small charge on currency transfers would calm damaging speculation while simultaneously raising huge sums for development.

people of highly developed democracies and thus even more so for people who still struggle with governance. Tobin taxes, once collected, must be handled by present balances of global power and according to presently-adhered-to global economic policies. The money from Tobin taxes would be used to finance development assistance for poor countries, and so the existing inefficiencies will only multiply by adding extra money.

Prerequisite for effective international relations of aid is the awareness of people of the kind of economy they want and responsibility of governments for people's needs. These two together must empower national policies first. Must a nation avail of capital before it can assert its power? Must there first be industry and trade and must the military be mighty? No, in a world of interdependent existence the deep truth is that power lies in life itself. All nations should take heart at the insight that their very existence and that of their people is the basis of their power. National policies that assert the existence of their people and the way they want to live are the dynamics of power in this world. And balance of power is the dynamic of peace in this world. The dynamics of large amounts of capital without self-awareness of people and assertive policies of nations only increases existing trends: misdistribution and bureaucratic inefficiency, imbalanced economies, and no world peace.

So if we do not like the Tobin Tax, then what does interdependent economy has to say about this misdirected money that speculation sends around the globe? It simply says, "capital that pays is capital that stays." Between economies with different strength of currency the weaker economies should keep capital, once sent in, inside their systems for a while. Capital can only do its work of improving quality of life over longer terms of time. Capital that does not stay does not make economic sense. Profits made on capital should stay in order to pay the people that created the profit with a betterment of their quality of life. Such stringent investment and money policies will definitely result in less foreign capital coming in, but should we see that as a curse or as a blessing? True economic blessings come from capital that builds up slowly from within and that is distributed evenly among the people of the land. Such inherent development is a gradual process and cannot be bought with capital that hits and goes, taking back the profits to where it came from.

The benefits of free capital movement between economies and currencies of similar strength must not be confused with the quick profits that can be made by the existence of structural inequalities between economies. In the latter case the quick profits are for the stronger party, while the long-term losses of instability are for the weaker one. The sum total for the world is more poverty and less world peace.

Policymakers of all currencies, weak and strong, should say, "let us look at where the capital goes and what it does." Then with quality of life as the guiding principle they may reflect on policies that must give some steering. Not taxing but completely barring operations that are speculative is the right policy. I already explained that speculative profits may be logic from the individual's point of view, but in the total of societal value they make no economic sense. To focus the restrictions on amounts above a certain measure may make it feasible to operate such policies, be they national or international.

To pass judgment on the good of international investments that produce and put people to work is a matter of fine-tuning. Universal standards are hard to set; the ideologies of the societies (not the companies!) who invest may not coincide with the interests of the people who can get jobs. Safety and green standards do not always sound the same for all. I cannot conclude this discussion here, but let me just put forward what, from the point of view of policy, international investment should be about. It is the interest—that is, the gradual improvement of life's circumstances—of those who have less choice. And what about profit? The individual investor will guard his interests, and so policy can be at rest.

Macro-policies on capital and investment are complex in their detail, but the overarching guideline is simply this: hold the value of more fractured capital distribution dearer than ever-growing capital concentration in few places. The latter is the natural outcome of many micro-agents following their micro-logic, and we cannot blame them for not seeing the balance in toto. It is the same adage as we used before: to spread risk is to minimise risk. And we add another saying: prevention is better than cure. Commonplace it is, but also specially true for international financial crises. I do not need to argue further to show that continued increase of capital concentration does not guarantee continual increase of quality of life.

12. Banks for Development—Long Gone Bankrupt

Let's face it: the World Bank—by any standards of commercial banking—has long gone bankrupt. Its debtors are heavily indebted and massively default. The efficient consequence to be drawn from this fact is that its business—developing the world—has been a fiasco.[1] However, the World Bank is not maintained by commercial results, but by political interests. These interests stay in business as long as the clout of the financiers remains. It is exactly the financiers' policies that corrupt any possibility of true, inherent development of the receiving nations and societies. So, twice bankrupt, financial and political, an institution is beyond repair. I care to not omit acknowledgment of the sincere efforts by many World Bank staffers who work hard and truly intend to help countries and their people. But their intentions must stay within the politics that really rule where the money goes and what it does.

Let us dwell a little on the coming into being of the World Bank. After World War II the Bank, or really the International Bank for Reconstruction and Development (IBRD), was established (1945) to help finance the reconstruction of war-torn Europe. Now that is exactly the crux of the matter. To finance the reconstruction of a physical infrastructure that was in place before and that harmonised with concurrent societal and political structures is one mandate. But to develop a society that does not have the characteristics of a capitalist economy is another one. Capital injection is the main instrument of the Bank, of any bank, and it fitted well the European mandate after World War II. But, though money may be needed, capital is not the tool for development. Capital can finance roads or production plants, but it does not buy development. Unfortunately, institutions rarely phase themselves out when their function has ceased to exist. They have the tendency to "hang in there" and go in search for new life like a predator

---

1. For an in-depth investigation into the World Bank's policies and comprehensive research on its projects see Catherine Caufield, *Masters of Illusion, the World Bank and the Poverty of Nations* (London, 1998).

for its prey. And so, the IBRD was seconded by the International Development Association (IDA, 1960) that extends concessional loans[2] to developing countries.

To my knowledge and astonishment the following contra-logic has gone unnoticed by both pro- and anti-World Bank contenders. The Bank prides itself on ever-increasing amounts of loans extended each year to countries in need of development. For any bank, indeed, to increase lending volume is to increase business, and this makes economic sense. For an agent of development, however, to increase assistance year after year to the same recipient is a sure sign that its business is failing, for if a recipient was truly going forward on its path of development he would need less and less.

It is like a father investing in his son's education who would proudly tell his friends about the end of his financial burdens because the son is now earning his independent way. If instead the son keeps failing his exams and the father is compelled to keep supporting him for years and years on end, the father would loudly complain or shamefully keep quiet about it. But he certainly would not proudly flaunt the figures of his expense. The mere fact that the Bank has the instinct of a bank and sees its interest in the increase of lending volume is in itself the exact wrong window through which to see development. Development comes from people's own indigenous resourcefulness, and untimely capital kills just that. World Bank loans have been forced on developing countries for projects they did not want, they did not need, and certainly could not afford.

Development, like the growing up of children, may need money but not loans. Money for development should be given, and capital can be loaned where sufficient productivity has already developed. If it were the policy of parents to ask back the money spent on educating their child, he could never grow up to become an independent adult. He would have to remain economically crippled for life. Development, therefore, does not need a bank but an institution of money distribution. It also needs people's self-awareness of the kind of economy they want and it needs their government's economic policies that reflect exactly that. The natural instinct of the World Bank to increase its lending volume is the sure cause of the phenomenon of Heavily Indebted Poor Countries (HIPCs).[3]

---

2. Concessional loans by IDA are loans at zero interest with a ten-year grace period and maturities of 35 to 40 years.

3. There are now officially 42 HIPCs. Their debt stocks to the World Bank rose from U.S. $0.6 billion (1970) to U.S. $39.6 billion (1999). Their total debt stock rose from U.S. $6.7 billion (1970) to U.S. $205.3 billion (1999). (Source: www.worldbank.org/hipc/).

Formerly only poor, now these countries are poor and burdened with unbearable debts.

My oration here just names the World Bank. But let it be an archetypal name for all other development banks and lending programmes which work along the same pattern as this global bank. Interdependent economy does not have much to say about the future of these banks. With the focus on people's true needs of livelihood I say cut the losses, file for bankruptcy, and close the business. World institutions that are policy agents of one way of life, of one kind of economy, have no place in a world of cultural diversity—the true wealth of the people of this world.[4]

---

4.   The ASN Bank in the Netherlands, a bank for socially and environmentally sustain-able investment, has excluded the World Bank (and the European Investment Bank) from its bond portfolio. ASN's August 2003 Newsletter says: "Since too many neg-ative effects on the environment and local population still exist for many large-scale projects of the WB, for now, the WB remains excluded."

13. *The International Monetary Fund*

The other world bank, the International Monetary Fund (IMF), does not deal in development. Its mandate is a different one; it is the mandate of keeping world financial operations smooth and currency reserves in balance. But as the IMF spreads its wings over developed and developing economies alike, its policies are bound to affect development as well. The IMF even designed special policies for poor countries. Programmes of budgetary austerity are laid upon governments of countries that are spoilsports in the international game of money and trade. Their balance of payments is negative; their reserves of foreign currency are insufficient. They cannot pay for foreign imports and even less for foreign debts. It is beyond the capacity of this simple paragraph to try and analyse the history by which such imbalanced situations came about. However, serious and structural imbalances in currency traffic between one economy and the other must be rooted in serious and structural imbalances between the two economies, that is, in their productive power.

The austerity programmes of the IMF want to enforce realignment between economies of unequal strength while weakening the weak economies even further. Who is at fault, the IMF or the governments that do not stand up for their interests? Let's not blame them or us. Let's choose better policies; not policies that prioritise foreign money operations and create no wealth for people but policies that take care of people and their basic needs.

Seventy percent of the world's poorest people live in rural areas and depend on agriculture.[1] Millions of poor city dwellers must survive on micro-business, and micro loans[2] could save their lives. It does not take a genius mind to understand that their economic interests do not lie with free currency exchange and free trade with the foreign countries of the OECD.[3] Their immediate livelihoods depend

---

1.   UNDP, *Human Development Report 2003*, p. 4.
2.   Microcredit is a development strategy employed to fight poverty. The system has been developed in the 1970s by Mohammad Yunus, Bangladesh. Loans can be as small as U.S. $50,-.

on small-scale production and markets they can oversee. Foreign money may be needed to finance further development and international trade. But money policies without people's inherent productivity in view are in themselves mere drawings on water. The ripples of such empty policies only disturb people's lives, sometimes very violently, and never sustain them. Finance can be planned with a view on people's self-empowered progress, and these are policies that have real substance.

For countries of low but similar levels of economy it would be economic wisdom to unite and thus broaden the base for development of trade and formation of capital among peers. Unfortunately, barriers of politics and barriers on roads are often in the way of unity and cooperation. Faced with such real hindrances at home, does it make sense to flee into financial dreams that come from another economic world? Control is the indispensable condition when introducing capital to further economic growth. Policymakers should relinquish foreign capital rather than have people lose control over their own economic resources and thus over their livelihoods.

Let us turn to the people of high economies and high democracies: the people of the countries of the OECD. Their contributions to the IMF weigh heavy, and therefore they can exert control. Maybe the people should start to make some inquiries and demand accountability from their governments. And maybe they will reformulate their mandate. After all, we institutionalised 2700 or so IMF economists to dictate economic terms to 1.46 billion people.[4]

---

3. Organisation of Economic Cooperation and Development. The OECD is a group of 30 countries including all developed economies.

4. Noreena Hertz, *The Silent Takeover, Global Capitalism and the Death of Democracy*, London, 2001, p. 258.

PART II
A FRAMEWORK FOR IMPLEMENTATION

In the second part of this book we unfold some marking points for policy implementation. These are to be understood as mere fundamental principles of problem analysis and strategy formulation. They are not the outline of a utopian society or model economy. On the basis of the same fundamental concepts and views of interdependent economy different people with different life styles and value systems can build very different economies and societies. By relying on a set of basic but universal economic principles and not on an image of some perfect end, societies can retain flexibility for change and gain development potential.

1. True Needs of People—A Practical Notion for Policy?

Until now we have placed the fulfillment of needs of livelihood central in our discourse. This is quite justified, because all of us deal with this reality day by day. But it is also true that for the macroeconomic policymaker it remains an ephemeral entity. We have seen that our needs must be determined by dynamic societal processes and that awareness of our true needs is often eclipsed by the needs of growth policies or clouded by cultural confusion. So how can such vague notions give us guidelines for concrete policies and actions? To answer this question I will first complicate the issue still more…and then, surprisingly, we will start to see more clear.

When we hear the term fulfillment of our economic needs we naturally think of the consumption of all kinds of goods and services that sustain our lives. But in the reality of people's economic life, the fulfillment of needs is not only consumption, but also production and distribution. In all of these aspects of the economy people's needs are expressed and must become fulfilled. It is in the inter-woven fabric of production, distribution, and consumption that we live our inner-felt values about relatedness, about caring and sharing, about individualism or cooperation, and about personal growth or living a life of selfless service. There are cultures—and thus economies—where sharing with one another is emphasised, and there are cultures—and thus economies—where keeping for oneself is emphasised. This book is not about making moral judgments; it is about bringing to the fore the interdependent nature between economy and the human culture that is expressed in it. It is in this cycle of production and consumption, with distribution as a natural link between the two, in which people live their economy while expressing their way of life. People will fulfill their needs as they partake in this cycle. What policymakers therefore must do is *keep people involved* in this cycle of the economy and leave no one out. Furthermore, it is not just keeping people involved that is the mandate, but also to keep them involved at modes of *sustainable quality*. This means that man and nature can regenerate from the wear and tear that economic activity naturally brings along. A worker who must work but cannot feed himself and his family, cannot seek cure when he is sick, cannot survive when he is old, and cannot give his children the necessary education they need to go on living, is spending his productive force but is not allowed to regenerate. An economy that produces and consumes but does not ensure the ongoing quality of the natural habitat we must live in and live of endangers future life.

So here we bring in two factors into the equation of what is sound economy that were not there before—*people* and *quality*—whereas before we only knew aggregated figures of Gross Domestic Product. The latter are figures on mere quantities of money; they leave us in the dark about the quality of the economic life of people.

2. The Creation of Our Wealth—Free Market or State Intervention?

It is the quest for more and better economic life that seems to confront mankind with the choice between two goods: more policy intervention or more laissez-faire.[1] Going back in the history of European economic policy we come across the state's protectionist measures of mercantilism, the free market of early capitalism, the centralised systems of communism, the welfare state of socialism, and the neo-liberal policies of global capitalism. Each of these models for the economy implies the struggle between two parties in society: those who want more state and those who want more liberty. Now how do we stand on this?

Interdependent economy proposes as the aim and focus of economic policy the sustainable involvement of all people in the cycle of production and consumption. Is there a role for free market forces to play, or must this all be orchestrated by state intervention? It is not a matter of ideology to believe in the preponderant role of the market mechanism to keep the economy going. It is mere observation of reality to state that the meeting of supply and demand through the intermediary of price—for this is what the market is—brings goods and services to people in a satisfactory way. It is a mechanism that quite effortlessly—so it seems—strikes a balance between the individual's need for free choice and the societal good of efficient distribution. This mechanism comes so effortlessly in motion by the spontaneous activity of individuals, and laissez-faire therefore is its best policy.

But it is this phrase saying "the spontaneous activity of individuals" that requires some more investigation. This phrase says that the free forces of the market mechanism require *individuals* in order to do their efficient work. I consider it understood that these individuals must have some ability and some productive power. It really only needs very basic intellect to see that incapacitated and disem-

---

1. Laissez-faire is the term used for an economic policy of minimal state intervention and maximal freedom for citizens.

powered people will not produce, will not sell, cannot earn, and therefore will not buy. Therefore, without able and empowered people there can be no efficient markets. And really, it is people who make markets. It is not markets that make people. Whether it needs more than basic intellect to understand the latter statement, I am not sure. But some policies that preach the foremost value of free markets seem not to be aware of this. They say that we must promote free markets in order to fight poverty of people. Interdependent economy says: there is no efficient market mechanism when people are too poor to consume and too weak to produce.

Macroeconomic policies, therefore, that want to fulfill the needs of people must keep them involved in the cycle of the economy—production and consumption. Where people lack strength and productive power, policy intervention must promote that first. Where people are temporarily or structurally unfit to produce, policy intervention must allow them to consume at basic levels at least. Only then markets will fulfill their function, and efficiently bring to people what they need as by "an invisible hand."[2]

Let me repeat this just once more: the final operational lead for economic policy is to bring good health, social strength, and productive power to people where it does not yet sufficiently exist, and to maintain and safeguard these qualities, if necessary, in addition to people's own capacities to do so. With that policy task being fulfilled, healthy, strong, and empowered people will indeed spontaneously form markets, and the mechanism can do its work.

And then there was another word I used when saying "market," I said "price." Now this is the very clue of the market mechanism, and therefore prices must be right. For a policy mandate qualified by sustainability, this means that prices must reflect all costs of regeneration from wear and tear. Prices must include the cost of labour that is allowed to regenerate itself, and prices must reflect the prudent use of natural resources. Without such proper prices markets may fulfill the immediate needs of some, but the needs of others who must labour too cheaply and the needs of generations that still must come are not served by the market mechanism when prices are not right.

---

2.   This alludes to the well-known concept by Adam Smith in his *Wealth of Nations* that the self-interested behaviour of man will make markets function efficiently without the need for state intervention; as if God intervened with an "invisible hand."

Well, let us have no illusions on this point: the micro-logic strongly goes in search of lower prices. End-users, and therefore also the producers, all hold dear the benefit of cheap and cheaper still. Policies that want to calculate right prices will fail for want of popularity. The least we must do, however, is to acknowledge fair and square that markets are not yet efficient as long as we are not willing to pay the proper price. Policy should bring loud and clear to our consciousness where and when costs will arise, and who must pay the price for present inefficiencies. Clarity on such facts may help to bring about the political will of both the public and policymaker to opt for long-term responsibility instead of short-sighted anxiety.

"Efficiency of markets and prices should be right" does not exclude the instrument of price regulation and subsidy. With a view on fulfilling people's needs by supporting their health and their inherent productivity, prices of certain goods and services may need to be reduced. Such policies redistribute the paying of the costs; they do not leave costs unpaid.

In conclusion of this paragraph on market versus policy-intervention I summarize as follows. The free forces of the market mechanisms will, by its basic nature, do fine at keeping people involved in the economy. But policy intervention must see to it that all people qualify for participation in the market. This means that policy must begin with securing basic livelihood and must support, if needed, the development of basic productive skills. What policy clearly must not do is disturb existing livelihoods and destroy productive activity that is already there. What seems so logic when we write it down is sometimes hard to implement in the reality of life. What often happens when economies of different levels meet is that the economy of the one takes away the life of others. And this happens sanctioned by official policy.

Therefore free markets must know another pre-condition, for free market is competition. And as in sports, some win…some lose. But we only enjoy the game when players are of the same league; lightweight against heavyweight does not make an interesting match. In the same way markets must match their players. Only then is the game good and the mechanism efficient. When this pre-condition is not given, a nation's policy must provide additional protection so its people stand a chance. Or, if such measures cannot be, then governors should call off the game and focus on building strength of inner markets first. To understand these necessary pre-conditions for markets to be free is to see the invisible hand as Adam Smith meant it to be.

3. The Measure of Good Economy—Money or People?

We will have to dwell on how to measure policies that go by the lead of people and quality, for policies need measures and yardsticks for direction and evaluation. Growth policies go by the measure of total output, that is, statistics on Gross Domestic Product (GDP) or Gross National Product (GNP).[1] But for other policies we will need other statistics.

Whereas the micro-unit aspires after individual growth in quantity and quality, macro-policy must aim at keeping all people involved in the economy—and that is quantity. Macro-policy must also safeguard the sustainability of that involvement—and that is quality. If these are the two foci of policy, then these are what we must measure. By using our imagination, we can already understand here that the dynamics of such People/Quality statistics will be quite different from those of GDP statistics. Data on output make policies focus on output; data on people make policies focus on people. And so we see that a simple device from just a supportive discipline can drive policies towards or away from people. Statistics can inform us about the fulfillment of people's needs or create a smoke screen of only secondary information.

Now how do we go about setting up such People/Quality statistics? First each society must set its own minimum standards of livelihood depending on its own level of development and its own life's values. There is no universal standard that must be the measure for all. Then statistical data gathered are set against these standards, and thus evaluation can take place. To know if all people are involved in the economy and at levels of sustainable quality, we count those who do *not* meet the standards. Therefore the measure taking by People/Quality statistics is a negative one: the less the better.

---

1. GDP and GNP are the most frequently used indicators of a nation's wealth. Gross Domestic Product counts all production generated domestically. Gross National Product adds to this income payments received from abroad and subtracts income payments made to abroad. The difference between GDP and GNP is irrelevant for the discussion in this book. See Appendix D on "Counting People's Wealth."

For the People indicator or the measure that tells us if people are involved in the economy, a minimum standard must be set, below which we consider people as "not involved." "People" here are not just those in the age bracket of the workforce but also the aged and children. All of them should be involved, each group in its own way.

For the first group, the people of working age, involvement is not narrowed down to income from work, employed or independent. Receiving income from (social) insurance schemes also counts as keeping them involved. In many economies, to restrict counting to income of the monetary kind would seriously distort the picture; access to land or other ways of remuneration in kind are important means of survival. Not to consider these non-monetary strategies of life will declare people poor who are not. Worse, however, is the consequence that policies will err on solutions. Well-intended development policies may emphasise monetary solutions while ignoring more appropriate, non-monetary strategies.

Involvement in the economy for those who are too old to work—and in some places people can never be too old to work, they just work until they die—can be determined by the inclusion in pension schemes or in family or community care. Again, whatever a society decides that their standards must be, whoever does not meet these standards must count as "not involved."

What do we mean by economic involvement of children? Not child labour of course, although in some places the earnings of a child maintain the family. Economic policy for children is to give them education and to train their skills in accordance with the survival strategies of their community. Learning the alphabet is said to be a universally-needed skill, and it probably is. But is it always economically wise to take children far away from their homes to learn from books that will never feed their families? It is not for me to answer this question. I just want to trigger the awareness that economies are multi-variable and people must know their own needs. To build infrastructure that is nearby where children learn skills needed to build their own communities is certainly an option next to building schools of learning far and high; that is, if we want to keep the economy going. Policy evaluation proceeds in the same way: set the minimum standard and count those who fall below. Whether one minimum standard suffices or whether one wishes to be informed by steps of standards is a further detailing I will not enter into now.

What policies must be made for those who are not involved? Again, there is no standard answer. But if no immediate individual solutions can be found, then policy must respond and provide at least some kind of minimum livelihood. Must this always be state provision, or can civil cooperative activity be employed? Must the benefits extended always be monetary or can they be in kind? Must we only fill gaps of consumption or should there be equal emphasis on training skills and improving structures? Policymakers would do well to look at all these aspects and also at combinations of them. Different societies at different levels of development and with different economies can come with different solutions.

What we see here is the immediate effect of People statistics on the focus of policy solutions. Statistics on growth of production will only lead us to want more production, but not to sustain the people who must produce. Statistics that inform us that people are not involved in the economy will lead us to want to know who and why and what strategies must be followed to reverse that situation. Interdependent economy tells us that policies following the lead of "better people make better economies" make more sense than policies saying, "free markets give us growth."

And now let us take a look at the Quality indicator or the measure informing us on people's sustainable involvement in the economy. How do we go about that? We have defined sustainability as the ability to regenerate from the wear and tear the economy naturally brings along. Again, each society must set its own standards that are both responsible and feasible. But here follow some universal questions that must be answered. Are working conditions safe enough or too hazardous? And let us remind ourselves that in the private home much is produced for livelihood, so here conditions should be safe as well. In some societies this means that we must especially take care of the conditions in which women do their work. Then, do all people have access to medical care? Are all children in the care of parents or other caretakers? Are all elderly people taken care of by either family or friends or in institutions? Can people, young and old, spend enough leisure time? And is the quality of our natural environment prudently guarded? Again here, the reality one measures is set against the standards that fit a particular community, culture, or country. Underperformance triggers and leads the policies.

Such People/Quality information held against the light of the minimum standards that were set beforehand will change the dynamics of policies dramatically. Information on numbers of people falling below standards or on quality failing minimum standards will immediately draw attention to the problem areas where policies must be focused. Compared to this, the information on mere figures of growth are bland. In order to design policies that nurture the inherent productivity of people, the authorities must either command further research or must wait for people to voice their concerns…and some people's voices are never heard.

Let us look at one example: America. If instead of high-profile publicity on the rate of growth of GDP, the U.S. Department of Economic Affairs were to prominently publish data on the number of people that live below the line of poverty, on the qualitative conditions of this poverty, and the budget needed to remedy the situation, and these matters were put forward as priority economic issues, then the effect on U.S. policies might be considerable. Maybe the war on domestic poverty would win over the war on foreign targets. Domestic issues could become so urgent in the public eye that popular support for costly foreign military operations might dwindle before the Administration's very eyes. Instead, hope for some 35 million Americans (12% of total population) who now live below the U.S. poverty line (approx. U.S. $17,000 p.a. for a family of four) has dwindled to very low expectations.[2]

Now some may feel that the aspects of People/Quality statistics are a matter of social policy or even are moral issues. Some economists may start to feel uneasy, because we now tread unfamiliar terrain. But all that interdependent economy argues is that if we want to produce good output and sustain our productive force, economic policy must be directed towards ensuring good productive input, and wear and tear must be repaired. Healthy and productive people who can live in a wholesome habitat are the deeper causes of a stable and balanced cycle of the economy. To narrow-mindedly focus on production in monetary terms only will never give us a real grip on the economy but continue to confront us with drop-outs and instability. Today's economics of mere money growth may work well for some, but for many just along a downward spiral. And yes, it is a matter of morality to want to look at the deeper causes why this is so.

There is still another virtue of the People/Quality statistics, namely that of befitting different cultures and different levels of economy, for standards are not set "one-fits-all" but contextually. In contrast, the present practice of GDP statistics fits only one: a strongly monetized economy. Here growth induced in some few sectors can bring economic opportunity throughout society facilitated by all-pervading markets that make this money go around. But billions of people in this

---

2.   The official Welfare Budget of the U.S. government is $24 billion a year (AFDC Program). This equals the Pentagon budget for four weeks (www.worldhunger.org). Cost estimates for the invasion in Iraq and the aftermath reconstruction are between $40 to $200 billion. Source: *The Waste Basket*, September 20, 2002: "Weighing the Costs of Invasion" (www.taxpayer.net).

world live by way of self-sufficient production, by an economy of barter, or by activities in the informal economy. Their economic worlds are not permeated by money flows that cycle in the formalised sector. Their economic empowerment is not increased by business induced by foreign currency. For sectors of the economy where money and markets are less prone, GDP statistics are non-informers as to the state of people's economic life. And for true economic policy, it is the latter that must count. People/Quality statistics will give each society the quality information that their policymakers need. It is the information that resounds with the people's own survival strategies and that thus induces policies that support a people's own economy.

If the socio-economic dynamics of People/Quality statistics harness better focused and more truthful policies than those of GDP, then the essential question is: will there be a revolution of reason or will misinformation continue to reign? The answer is with us, the people of the world.

4. Two Pillars of Policy—All for Individuality

Until now, I have reasoned much and vehemently against the linear thinking of growth policies. I said this is a micro-logic; it is the interest of the one unit. And macro-policy, I said, must take care of the whole. So I shed light on the circular policies of fulfilling people's needs by keeping them involved in the cycle of production and consumption. However, interdependent economy never wanted to deny the vigour and life-sustaining energy of the micro-instinct that forever seeks to grow in quantity and quality. I just wanted to distinguish and not confound two separate lines of logic. But now it is time to bring things back in balance and make the picture whole.

Individual life is the beginning and end of all communality. It is our innermost desire for individual existence that gives meaning to all we do. This is not to say that all that the individual does is wholesome and right. However, the fault does not lie with individuality, but with lack of insight in what is wholesome and what is right. It is to make up for this lack of total knowledge that we sometimes need common regulation from above. But as we go about fulfilling our needs of livelihood it is the individual's sense of direction we rely on first and foremost. It makes sense therefore that common policy should treasure and nurture this individual's common sense. Now what exactly is this individual's common sense? How does it operate? It is freedom coupled with know-how and responsibility; let us call that maturity. It is this individual's freedom plus maturity that is the mainstay of our livelihood that otherwise no policy, however wise, can organise to come around. Now, from this short excursion into philosophy proclaiming that individuality must be the end of all policy, we go back to economics.

Within the framework of keeping all people, and that is each individual person, involved in the cycle of the economy at levels of sustainable quality, we will now detail two further aspects of policy. These are no minor details but two important pillars of policy implementation. The one pillar is to secure basic existence for all; the other pillar is to take care of common matters that arise when many individuals go about their economic business. The policy for the first pillar we already explained: it is to keep all people inside the boundaries of minimum standards of involvement in the economy. All strategies made to accomplish this end concern the first pillar of securing a basic existence for all. Why is this first pillar part of a policy for individuality? Because without basic life, without bare survival, there is no existence. And who can argue with the fact that mere existence is the minimum pre-condition for any form of individuality?

But then some will wonder: what about the interests of commerce and industry, the main concerns of economic policy as we think of it today? Does interdependent economy neglect these activities that really make and trade all that we need for livelihood? Yes. And with good reason, because if it is the individual's freedom and maturity we want to further, then intervening with policy is not the strategy we need. And who can argue with the fact that freedom coupled with maturity is the essential seed for further growth and development of individuality?

But how can we simply neglect such important activity, something we constantly occupy ourselves with as if it is not our second, but our primordial nature? Well again here, it is the micro- and the macro-logic confused. It is the individual who will worry about production and distribution, driven of course by his constant need for consumption. It is not the fundamental worry of macroeconomic policy to produce, distribute and make people consume. The individual can be trusted to do the job; it is indeed his nature. Once basic security is laid as a foundation, individuals will quite naturally seek to increase their wealth; they will seek to produce, to trade, to be employed, and to consume in ever new and better ways. No policy is needed to instil such instincts in mankind. And if the individual has reached the limits of his satisfaction, for what good shall policy induce him to want more? Therefore I say, neglect is the best policy.

But when many individuals busy themselves in all kinds of economic activity, there are externals that arise. By this I mean societal effects connected with the individual's behaviour and for which the individual does not assume responsibility. He does not do it because he either cannot do it or does not want to do it. Externals could be facilitating conditions for the activities of production and consumption, or negative effects coming from these. They can be the construction of roads or other works of infrastructure, the delivery of communal services, or the regulation of industrial sites. They can be making legislation on prices or labour relations. They can be cleaning up waste or taking measures to diminish dangerous emissions and so on. All these harmonising activities that are necessary to connect the economic behaviour of many individuals into one well-working whole is the second pillar of macroeconomic policy for governments to undertake.

But all the strategies of this second pillar should be designed and executed with the sole intent of organising the externals that individuals will not do. They should not be done in the vein of favouring the business of production or pushing the level of consumption. The correct order is policy should favour people, and people will push industry and commerce. Therefore, subsidising mature industry (big money goes there now mostly hidden from the public eye) is not a policy intervention supported by interdependent economy. Instead, it favours a second realm of liberal economy for individuals based on a primordial space of economic security for all. The judgment where to draw the exact dividing line between these two levels of economy, and thus between the two pillars of policy, will change with time and place. But at a given time and place, to first clearly define the minimum standards that policy intervention wants to secure for all will then leave us with the economic space where liberty and responsibility are for the individual's choice.

There is a great advantage in making clear distinctions and setting well-understood priorities: we avoid the mistake of totally confused policies. Subsidising mature industry and letting people pay for basic goods at prices they cannot afford are both measures taken now with the view of implementing good economy. But both are totally inefficient in fulfilling our needs. The one does not fulfill the need for basic livelihood, something that we all must have. The other does not fulfill the need for liberty and individual responsibility for things that we can have.

And so I will condense this paragraph into the following short piece of advice. We now speak of a world that is divided into two: the haves and the have-nots. It is much better to divide economic strategy in two: of *must-have* and of *can-have*. Let policy secure what all must have, let the individual's ability take care of what we can have.

5. *To Gain Productivity Is to Lose the Hard/Soft Policy Divide*

Interdependent economy commands to keep all people involved in the economy, including those who cannot work. Is this the welfare state? To some this is a welcome term that feels like security and care. To others it is the horror of profiteering people and Moloch governments. The focus that I propose, however, is sharply on increasing the inherent productivity of individuals, but without the narrow-mindedness of equating growth of GDP with good economy. The lead of "people's productivity"—and in this book I always mean to say productivity that is inherent[1]—will have a strange effect on our view of what is the domain of economic policy. It has the effect of lifting from our minds the divide between soft social sectors and hard economic issues.

In present policies there is much cushioning of industry, and people must pull hard to bend policies their way. Let us take note that in some countries we subsidise farmer millionaires and pamper dairy cows.[2] Is it macro-economically efficient to pay for private business interests that are already fully mature and thus facilitate surplus production the world does not need? Soft measures for hard sectors is a combination that is bound to kill the economic life of others that still must grow. This interdependent relation is always true, but in particular at global scale we can now observe its painful effect on economies that still must grow.

So what are the sectors that are relevant for macroeconomic policy? When we take the broader view of sustaining people's productivity as the goal instead of narrow-mindedly focusing on growth of commerce and industry alone, then this is what we see. All such sectors like health care, education, housing, commonly needed infrastructure, as well as the sectors of industry and commerce will take their proper place in one coherent setting. Also, to focus on increasing people's productivity will help us to avoid pamper policies that overindulge in providing for individuals by state programmes and benefits. Such policies stem from senti-

---

1.　See Part I, Chapter 5, footnote 1 for definition of inherent productivity.
2.　See Appendix E on "Agricultural Policies and Poverty."

ments that sympathise with weakness. But inherent productivity, clearly, is not weak; it is empowerment. We used the phrase before: people's inherent productivity is the essential money that buys wealth. So all sectors of policy, when they are bent on furthering people's inherent productivity, become sectors of the economy—be their feel one of care and share or their push for better individual performance.

Therefore, to further people's inherent productivity is the final practical notion that can lead policies even in the midst of ignorance. We do not always have the infrastructure for building complete statistics. We do not always have full market information. Our methodologies and know-how are not always state-of-the-art. In the reality of our lives, there is more we do not know than what we know. But often we do know what must be done to increase people's productivity in the immediacy of here and now. We must always provide food when people lack nutrition and we must never destroy production potential and markets that people need. Sometimes we must let in foreign competition when monopolies grow inefficient. At times we must increase efficiency of civil servants, and at other times we must induce self-responsibility of citizens. To forego such immediate action in search of something else is waste, and to waste is never good economy.

6. To Sum It All Up

So, with this I have defined the fulfilling of our needs of livelihood as the prime goal of macroeconomic thinking and policy. I have explained as its operational strategy the sustainable involvement of all people in the cycle of production and consumption—and these cycles can be monetized or non-monetized, and formal or informal. We have seen that people live different cultures, and that means living different modes of production, distribution, and consumption. Therefore ownership of economic resources by people of one culturally-coherent group must be at the top of the list when we respect cultural diversity. And finally I have placed individuality as the aim of all policy, implying that the operational lead for all economic policy can only be to further the individual's inherent productivity. This must be done by relying on two pillars of policy: first, the securing of basic needs fulfillment, and second, the regulation of externals, that is, measures that become the task of governance because the individual cannot take them on. To pursue growth levels above the basic standard is left to the individual's resourcefulness; here state intervention can be decreased to levels of laissez-faire. Pursuing the individual's inherent productivity brings us back to where we began—to fulfill the needs of people. It is the only rationale for macroeconomic policy. And to fulfill the needs of all people of all nations is the only rationale for global economic policy.

This circular thinking, and not linear growth, must be the mainstay of policy whether we must develop from poverty or contain an overheated economy; whether we think locally or globally. Growth policies dictate a straight line and promise benefits that—for the majority of the people on this globe—are always in the future. The circular thinking of interdependent economy acknowledges the needs of people's plurality in the here and now—it is the shortcut to world peace.

PART III

STEPPING STONES FOR INTERNATIONAL ECONOMIC POLICY

In Part III we take a few policy issues of international importance and discuss them in the light of interdependent economy. The list is not meant to be exhaustive, and many issues are left untouched. The views of interdependent economy want to lead to states of better balance. And where are things more out of balance than in a world economy that leaves more than one billion of its people in a state of extreme poverty while at the same time material conditions to provide all with a life of dignity abundantly exist.

The consistent application of the principles of interdependent economy does lead to clear standpoints on strategies for action on any issue that is relevant in the reality of people's economic lives. Whether policymakers and planners are also willing to follow up on these strategies is of course less clear. But in the end it is the people's awareness of their choices that will cause them to no longer accept the status quo, and policies must change on popular demand.

1. The Economy of Arms—Take Out the Profit

There are some sectors in the economy where production and distribution cannot be left to follow the lead of private profit. There are some sectors of production where goods must be brought to where they are needed according to a scheme of common will and not by the system of the private purse. One such sector is weaponry and all technology of warfare, including its research and development.

Weapons and the like are clearly products that stand off from all other economic goods. They are means of last resort when existence is threatened to the core, and some think they should be completely banned. Here we do not venture into making judgments about the good or bad of the use of weapons. But it is safe to say that no civic man or woman will say, "the more the better, let production be abundant, let our nation thrive on the profits of the weapons' industry." Even governments and leaders that wield armies and plan to wage wars have an interest in restraint and regulation of the trade, lest the enemy obtains the weapons they themselves produce. The only party that has an interest in more without restriction is the one who garners the money profits on the production and sales of arms. So whatever one's stand on warfare and weaponry, the wish to control production and trade always accompanies the circulation of such destructive tools. The profit expectation is in direct opposition to such control.

I will not enter into the discussion of what systems of registration and transparency must be set up and how the fiscal details of such policies must work. For sure, at national and international levels regulation already exists. But as long as we leave the incentive of profit in the business, implementation of regulation will be like trying to catch a ghost. Its real movements cannot be followed and one never knows when and where the weapons will appear again.

So what I state here with great emphasis is that the profit sting must be taken out of the arms business. Profits of its trade and investment in its development must come under public rule. Such a proposition will meet with much resistance from the industry, of course, but also from the governors, including those of the military. Some say they are a team;[1] the one makes the weapons, the other makes the war, and so all profit in their own way. It is the people who always lose; therefore, it is from them that change must come. A first step towards this new strategy is to demand full transparency of who produces what, who buys, how much, and for what purpose. Publication of such facts together with expert comment on function and usefulness of the weaponry that goes around will at least facilitate informed opinions by the people on their economy of arms. After centuries of nation building, most of the nations' people now stand up for democracy as a universal good. But what is people's influence when it comes to undergoing war, a political event so invasive in their lives? Compared to that the many other issues they democratically discuss become mere trivialities.

We may not be able to do away with markets for weaponry, but fiscal legislation can seize the profits. We can set up structures that give transparency to the public eye and thus allow the common will to rule the economy of arms. And who knows, by such device and by public command, money made with destruction can be turned into a force for peace.

---

1.   We refer here to the Military-Industrial Complex (MIC), a network of high-ranking individuals from the military, the world of finance, the industry, and political hawks. These individuals use their political, administrative, and economic power to promote the development of defence budgets, arms production, and trade. The MIC networks also include scientists who are heads of research laboratories and who specialise in military research. (Andrée Michel, "The Military System and Violence against Women," in: *Connections*, March 1997. Andrée Michel is honorary chair of the Centre National de Recherches Scientifiques (CNRS), Paris.)

2. The Economy of Food and Medicine—Take Out the WTO

Food

Food production, and especially that which is basic and comes in bulk, is commonly felt to have the task of feeding us and keeping us alive. To produce food for profit is saying that food will go where the money is, which is the same as saying that no food will go where people cannot buy. The rulers of the world should take a moment to think about this consequence when they set their market policies on food production and distribution.[1] Self-sufficiency is the basic structure for food policies, for in matters of basic need one wants to keep control. Production and trade must be led by need profiles of the consuming population and not by profit interests of the producers. We must produce what we need and not eat what must be marketed by industry.

And then there is another quality to the production of food: reliable estimates say that 70% of the world's poorest people live in rural areas and depend on agriculture.[2] The sorry plight of millions of farmers in poor countries stands against the billions of dollars that subsidise inefficient surplus production of only a few agricultural entrepreneurs in rich countries. Tens of thousands of farmers who, with their trade, intend to keep the world alive are now driven by forces of world trade to acts of desperation. The South Korean farmer that set himself on fire at the Cancun WTO meeting (Mexico, October 2003) was one example for the world to see, but he was just one of many who simply die unnoticed.

The world is heavy with the many reports that document this ludicrous reality of millions going hungry, while huge food stocks rot away or are being sold at foreign markets instead of feeding indigenous people. If Malthus[3] was still alive and witnessed this human disaster, he would say, "I told you so, but just a little differently." For those who go hungry and are malnourished, it does not make much difference whether they starve because of lack of food technology or

---

1. See Appendix E on "Agricultural Policies and Poverty."
2. UNDP, HDR 2003, p. 4.

because of wrong marketing of food technology; they just starve. For the responsible policymakers it does make a difference. Lack of technology to produce sufficient food to feed the world's population cannot be helped at short notice. Wrong world policies on food, however, can be changed as soon as the will is there. *The whole issue of basic food must be taken out of the WTO project immediately.* Food production, and especially that what is basic and comes in bulk, must not be marketed for profit; it must be managed for satisfaction.

Again, this book is not for spelling out the details of policies and strategies. The concrete realities on the ground are too multi-faceted, and we cannot even begin to grasp them here. But let us not leave this subject without listing at least some of the worldwide challenges of the management of food production as seen by interdependent economy.

Nations faced with the starvation and malnutrition of their people should redirect their agricultural policies toward self-sufficiency first and foremost. The appropriate strategies ranging from sustaining the most basic, small-scale farming to subsidising larger production must be implemented where relevant. Food buffers must be maintained to feed one's people and not exported to balance trade imbalances. The simple lead for all policy is to produce what people need and support productive power there where it is lacking.

Concerning trade in food commodities, governments should first promote and exploit local, national, and regional markets. They should go overseas only to find additional opportunity. They should not accept any food imports that will destroy local markets. They should not accept foreign technology that people do not need, do not trust, and cannot own. The benefits of the people's traditional knowledge on homegrown food and indigenous plants should accrue to them, and therefore this knowledge must be safeguarded.[4] If governors of people who

---

3.   Thomas Malthus, an English economist of the eighteenth century, advanced the theory that there was a natural limit to the growth of the economy. Growing prosperity would bring along growing population. Food production, however, was limited by constraints of nature. Starvation would then again undo the economic advancement. Of course, Malthus could not foresee the technological advancement in agricultural methods of the twentieth century. With the technology of today, sufficient food can be produced to feed the world's population. In fact the struggle is now with overproduction. Nevertheless, millions of people are malnourished and die of starvation due to the failure of national and international policies on food.

4.   I do not imply that patents on plants or seeds should be put in place for private corporations to exploit. I mean to say that a nation's wealth should accrue to the nation's people and national policies should ensure that.

seek a life in dignity do not take up their responsibility, then who in the world will?

As for world markets that have been the lifelines for certain agricultural economies for a long time, a major management effort is needed. International management must distribute basic levels of export quotas to the different countries and also regulate prices, such that economies have at least a basic security of outlet. Prices must be fair, and all costs of man and nature must be accounted for. How further distribution on such a world market must be organised and how reserves must be stocked are certainly points of debate and further investigation. Nevertheless we believe that the real challenge does not lie with the management issue, but with the political will to produce food for people instead of money.[5]

Another issue of food management is the containment of overproduction. At times this will require the reduction of export quotas that have been allowed to protect development. Developing nations, therefore, must be prepared for that and complacency in agricultural strategies just because basic levels of production have been secured would be short-sighted policy. At the mid- and longer term, dependency on the export of one or only few commodities must be avoided and should be counteracted with wise economic planning. However, to impose diversification on short notice on a developing economy that is still grappling with the basic subsistence of its people is certainly not wise policy.

And what must rich countries do? Is it still possible that taxpayers, well-educated and highly democratic, accept to pay for huge agricultural subsidies that make no economic sense?[6] It obviously is high time for a major information effort so people know for what they vote. If it is not in developed democratic nations that people can influence the policies, then where on earth will it be?

The natural consequence of implementing a policy of food self-sufficiency for poor countries and allocating to them guaranteed volumes of export is less demand for the surplus production of the high-tech bio-industry and agribusiness of the richer countries. This will bring down the issue of the enormous subsidies by industrialised countries for their agricultural sector to one of national concern instead of international contention, and that is exactly what it should be. These

---

5.   International commodity agreements on, for instance, coffee, cocoa, and sugar have been at place in the past. Certainly much can be learned from understanding the reasons why they failed.

6.   OECD countries provided U.S. $311 billion in subsidies to their agricultural sector (2001). Much of these are used to pay farmers' prices above world market prices and therefore have the effect of maintaining overproduction. (Devinder Sharma, "WTO and Agriculture: The Great Trade Robbery," 2003.)

nations will now be faced with the urgent need to reform (that is to reduce) their agricultural sector, and that is exactly what they should do.

It is clear that the food policies for people outlined here cannot unfold under the umbrella of the free-trade-for-profit paradigm. It is clear that this means exit for the WTO, but who on earth asked for this institution anyway?

Medicine

What has been said for food also applies to medicine and curing methods, including research into new and improved methodologies. Health is a basic need without which there is no beginning of human life and, consequently, no further human development. Health is not a commodity the consumer ponders on whether he will buy or not, weighing his choice against other goods of preference. Nationally and internationally, the provision of medicine and cure must be the subject of pondering for policymakers how to get the treatment to the patient. The market and its price mechanism cannot be trusted to get this all-important job done well simply because it is not only those who can pay who become sick.

At world level, where medicines are here and diseases there—take tuberculosis or malaria—the real challenge is with logistics and not with lack of material means. The world has mandated the World Health Organisation (WHO) to look after its health, but if it leaves so many millions still dying of a disease that can be treated with a simple cure, then how can we, the tax-paying and democratically-empowered people of this world, remain complacent?[7] Interdependent economy, not always favouring global institutions, does see some benefit in global structures to manage basic and much needed provision of health. Global structures must support regional ones that again will support national structures that again support local provision of health. Not only the production and distribution of medicines and curing methods, but also education and employment of doctors and nursing personnel must be supported by these structures. The management challenge here is to work both bottom-up as well as top-down. Needs must be expressed from bottom-up, curing methods that are globally available must be distributed from top-down.

---

7.   Tuberculosis still causes two million deaths a year and malaria one million. At the same time, affordable and simple cures and medicines are available to combat these diseases (UNDP, HDR 2003, p. 8).

As to profits and patents in the industry of health I say the following. Medicine and cure should not be like magic—only accessible to those who possess the secret formula of money. Health is a basic need of people, and, in a world that has demystified its policies, basic cure must be there for everyone. The rule that says, "no pay, no cure" should not reign the market of basic health. Instead true macroeconomic logic that says, "we must fulfill our need for life" must lead the policies.

Medicine is much the same as food—in fact food is the medicine against the disease of hunger—and free-trade paradigms do not give us the guarantee of efficient distribution. Let us free the schemes of the WTO and similar free trade agendas of the marketing of medicine. Let us instead take on the organisational task of finance and distribution of cure to people.

3. Global or Local—Where Is Our Choice?

Debate what is global

Global economy, like all economy, consists of the two aspects of production and consumption. When we debate the subject it is good to separate the discourse accordingly, whether we propagate or protest.

Globalisation of production grows in conditions of a world that has become one economic sphere. Capital can freely roam around to settle where costs are low and production facilities are conducive. It is the micro-instinct that travels in a wondrous world of transportation and communication technology and takes advantage of a fall in costs, be it labour, land, or states' fiscal policies. As such there is no harm in that; it is the natural dynamic of things, and losing investment here means gaining investment there. We already saw before that pursuing growth comes with the invitation of instability; so we make our choices and must not complain.

The harm that is felt, however, and protested by those who care for just and fair, comes with exploitative labour conditions and environmental damage occurring at the place where the investment goes, whereas these would be outlawed at the place where the money leaves. In that way globalisation accounts for a loss of wealth in the total picture of the world. Whether it must be national legislation, global agreement, or both that will amend such impoverishment in one place through movement between places must be discussed. What we should not omit is to inform the people about their rights. These rights are to demand amendment of the quality of labour and life and to propose the way in which this should be done. What we should not forget is to support the rights of local people by the global awareness of others who can democratically, but forcefully demand new policies that will right the wrong. When policy allows capital to go global, then democratic people must control the global policies. The micro-logic of enterprise will naturally exploit its possibilities. Macro-policy must narrow down the options to those that do not harm.

Globalisation of consumption brings on debates of quite a different nature. Monopolies and cultural homogenisation are often felt to be unwanted. Products from strong economies that go global are known to often leave local producers with no fair chance. And we must question the demand on transport infrastructure by products that must always travel here and there.

Let us start by singling out that kind of globalised consumption that does make sense. Where standardisation serves worldwide use—for instance, communication through the Internet—marketing of the very same product everywhere does certainly make economic sense. In that way Microsoft does a great service to mankind by creating one software we all use. And so do Global Systems for Mobile Communication, tiny chips and huge aeroplanes—in short, all these inventions of the human brain that can serve us all in the same way. They are appropriate items for globalised consumption. But one wonders if the same international stage must be reserved for products like cement and flowers, for plastic spoons and woollen socks. Certainly, some brands represent a way of life and some like China tea while others prefer American Coca-Cola. It may be an enrichment of our lives when we can have the diverse specialities of the world. But many products that reach us from faraway places do not remind us of any place at all.

Again the micro-logic is clear, the producer seeks large markets and desires the world as his playing field. Macroeconomic policy, however, that must oversee the whole should scrutinise if all this back and forth does not come with costs that are not internalised. Globalised consumption comes with much additional activity: transport, storage, currency transactions, and customs procedures just to name a few. Some call it employment opportunity and economic growth. Others call it pollution, the stress of too much traffic, and the instability of financial markets. Producing goods in distant places, including the transport back to where users buy, is much cheaper according to industry. But do we calculate the costs of too many decibels for people who live near airports, the loss of nature for railway tracks or for container sites at harbours? Do we account for polluted air and congested flows of traffic? When we welcome the employment and economic growth that comes from sending products around the globe, then we could simply create these desirable variables by sending all goods ten times from A to B and back again. Clearly, everyone will see this as economic nonsense. But sending goods from here to there without accounting for all costs is considered the wisdom of economic globalisation.

Some call this world a global village; that may be so, but the economic life of the majority of the six billion villagers is still very locally bound. For them, a local economy that is complete in itself is still the only stable basis for their lives. Therefore, to regain what is local is more than just some good advice. It is a must, not one of fancy fashion, but one for our world to survive.

Regain what is local

Given the urgency of the policies, I feel compelled to forego polite discussion, and simply list the necessary measures as if they were commandments coming down to us.

1. Developed economies must do away with subsidies, export credits, and all kinds of financial support of private enterprise operating in mature sectors. Such policies manipulate the market mechanism without achieving better total fulfillment of needs.

2. Economies that still need basic levels of development should promote trade that is local, national, and regional. They should open up their markets only for other nations with peer economies, that is, economies with an equal degree of capitalisation and levels of technology. Using surplus production and trade in this way induces growth for all participants and comes with less instability of markets and currency rates, compared to trade with highly developed countries.

3. Economies where people still lack basic livelihood must concentrate on the development of an inherent economy first. National economies of subsistence, manufacturing, and industry must be prioritised, and dependency on foreign capital must be avoided. National production and consumption must be subsidised if necessary to secure livelihoods. This implies that imports can be barred or regulated by instruments like import quotas, tariffs, or currency exchange restrictions.

4. Developing economies must weigh well their operations on world markets, be it for primary commodities or manufactured goods. The needs of the nation's own people must be fulfilled first, especially the need for food. This implies that export must be embarked upon only when surplus productive power exists.

5. When export opportunities are truly supportive of gradual inherent development, access to global markets must be negotiated allowing no or only partial reciprocity.[1] If access to other nations' markets is denied under such protective

---

1.   Reciprocity in trade negotiations is the term used to indicate that both partners must open up their national markets for each other and eliminate trade barriers like tariffs, quota or quality requirements.

conditions, it is better to forego earning foreign exchange than to destroy the basic economy a nation can own. It is by the latter that the people of a nation survive, even if only at basic levels. Regional cooperation with peer economies is really the first asset when gradually enlarging markets. These opportunities should not be neglected also when trading opportunities with industrialised countries open up.

6. Developing countries should concentrate on building infrastructures—physical and institutional—that people can own and understand. They should opt for simple and transparent institutions, use local material and technology if adequate, and make use of the good social values that are known in the society. Even if higher technology is available, they should only introduce it if people understand it and if its application gives them greater control. When building these infrastructures, they ought to avoid the need for foreign aid, mobilising domestic resources to the utmost. If foreign aid is absolutely necessary, these nations should demand gifts and grants without any strings attached. Productivity that must still develop cannot afford to lose the capital that was initially invested nor the earnings made with it.

7. Developing countries still lacking sufficient productivity should never take up loans and credits to finance projects of human development like educational or health programmes. These are not the kind of commercial projects that earn the capital and profits needed to pay back the loan.

8. Industrialised countries talking aid should therefore *give* part of their productivity for such human development...or not aid at all.

9. If capital is needed for expanding further economic activity, then developing countries should go for long-term venture capital. That is capital that shares loss and gain with the developing economy and that comes to stay. Large sums, therefore, will not easily be found. However, step-by-step development that is people-controlled does not need huge volumes at a time. Many but smaller sums for small-and medium-scale business ventures are what is needed here. Cooperation with partners, private or governmental, in more affluent countries should be sought in order to approach such capital.

10. Private investors in affluent countries should take up this task of building structures and institutions that facilitate small-and medium-scale capital transfers to developing economies, with or without government support.

The list is not exhaustive nor must it be followed to the letter. It is meant to reflect the gist of policies that want to regain what is local. Let me conclude with the following remark: policies that firmly foster economies that nations and their

people can own are also very right for building a global economy that will belong
to us all.

4. Regional Currency—Better Money to Fight Poverty

If we were to penetrate into the central issue of the global/local debate, or in other words, our concern with strong economic imbalances at world level, then what is it that we would hit? It is something poor countries badly want but hardly can obtain: the promised land of foreign currency. If governors of poor nations could be assured—by some divine agent—that they can dispose of an inexhaustible well of foreign currency, then they would certainly feel that all their troubles are over. Let us look at what rich nations do. The present neo-liberal policies[1] they prescribe for nations faced with poverty mainly aim at increasing their ability to acquire foreign currency. Well, foreign currency in itself is neither good nor bad; what is important though is what we must do to get it. When we allow currency to flow from one economy into the other, a bond is forged between the two. If one is strong and the other is weak then the automatic consequence is a bond of inequality; that is, one of the two will lose control and become dependent on the other.

Let us make a long story short and not tell about the dictate of development policies, the bias of trade policies, the crises of financial policies, and the politics of power policies. Let us just look at what we see in the years following World War II. What we see is that developing countries have continually experienced the vicissitudes of weakening currencies, devaluation, hyperinflation, growing debts, worsening terms of trade, and structural deficits of balance of payment. And why is that? Because injecting large amounts of foreign currency into an economy that has not yet developed sufficient productive power makes prices rise—this is inflation. Foreign currency often comes with foreign goods that distort domestic demand structures—this is destruction of productive infrastructure. Foreign currency must always return to where it came from and thus puts

---

1. Neo-liberal is the term that denotes the policies of late capitalism. The ideology implies that the interests of a capital-induced economy and of the capital owner take primordial status in economic policies.

pressure on currency rates, even more so when increased with interest—this is worsening the terms of trade. Large amounts of currency that have not previously been earned by a people's own hard work and a nation's own industry induces random and unproductive distribution—this is corruption. In their attempt to level with these problems, where have the poor countries arrived today? They have arrived at a state of still more dependency on foreign currency. Does this start to look like an addiction?

The strong economies with their strong currencies are not amused. Alas, they are tied to these poor ones for the bond was forged both ways. They send in the IMF to remedy the awkward situation. But all the IMF can do is administer more of the drug and continue the addiction. And can we blame the institution? No, for foreign currency is the only cure it has. So what we call structural adjustment[2] really means more effort to earn more foreign currency, more dependence on global processes, less control over one's own economy, less inherent development, less national sovereignty, and less empowerment of people. The problem only deepens, and a real cure is not in sight.[3]

Let us try to unravel the mystery of this infatuation with foreign currency. Faraway countries and foreign cultures have always had a mesmerising effect on the mind of man. Why use this phrase in a book that wants to speak about the logic of economics? It is because the magic of the foreign can be enriching when imagination is at play, but when we must build the structures of our basic livelihood, it is close to home that we must stay. I am afraid that too much imagination is now at play in policies for basic livelihood.

---

2. The IMF attaches to its financial assistance the obligation to install Structural Adjustment Policies (SAP) by the receiving countries. These imply stringent fiscal measures in order to balance budgets and stabilise currency exchange rates. These policies have proven to be disastrous for the domestic economy of developing countries, and in particular, the livelihood of their poorest citizens.

3. I here want to quote Wangari Maathai, the Kenyan leader who was awarded the Nobel Peace Prize in 2004. In her book *Bottle-necks of Development in Africa* (1995) she says: "What is the reason for this economic marginalisation and impoverishment of Africa? It is partly because many of them do not participate in formulating and implementing their development policies. Decisions which affect their economic and political life are made by others in foreign capitals in the company of few of their ruling elites. These are the policies and decisions which facilitate the siphoning of their wealth, literally from under their feet. In the process they are marginalised and disempowered economically, denied access to information, knowledge and resources and forced to over-mine their environment thereby, jeopardising even their future generations."

In other words, developing countries are faced with the nasty problem of mass poverty. They are told, and unfortunately also believe, that they can recover from this humiliating situation by the magic of foreign currency. So they take up loans, strain their meagre productive resources not for own needs but for exports in order to repay the loans, cut government spending meant to support one's people—though some of it was not well spent—to balance budgets in order to get more loans, sell commodities at losing world market prices in order to earn foreign currency, and export buffer stocks of food meant to feed one's people in order to pay off the loans. And so the vicious circle goes on and on—much imagination, but no recovery from poverty. The truth without imagination is that poverty can only be eradicated when people's own productivity is restored, maintained, and nurtured. To do this we do not need foreign currency at all, not one dime. All we need is to manage well the resources that we already own.

Developing countries, of course, do not only want to lift their people from the depths of poverty. Imagination tells stories of further growth and if foreign relations can provide aid, then at some point this is the way to go. But gifts and grants must pave the way before foreign loans and capital can come in. And on the way to forging bonds with long distance economies, it is worth investigating if one should not first stay in the company of peers. Did poor countries try to command a regional currency before delivering themselves to the dictate of countries whose currencies in economic terms are very far away? In the upward struggle to an unburdened exchange with U.S. dollars, Yen, and Euros, it may be worthwhile to first befriend economies of equal strength and share markets that are regional. It may be worthwhile to investigate if the creation of a common currency at regional levels can be of help. Do not industrialised countries derive their global strength from regional cooperation and common markets with economies that are close? Now this is one policy from abroad that developing countries can safely imitate.

So how do we treat the present addiction of weak economies to strong currencies? The honest advice is to kick the habit cold turkey. Some few will sweat with the withdrawal pains of this harsh treatment, and, yes, they are the ones that influence the policies. But millions who never are at the core of any policies will not get worse, and with new policies, not foreign but indigenous, will gradually improve. We may gaze at mesmerising Millennium Goals[4] and raise billions of foreign currency for the project, but without such drastic measures now, I am certain, the goals will not be of this millennium.

So let me recapitulate in case too much rhetoric obscured the simple point. There is no relation at all between the recovery from extreme poverty and the availability of foreign currency. Only when we can cut through the mystification of this untrue belief can we start full force to make and implement the policies that will bring simple, sometimes still hard, but dignified lives to all.

---

4.   The Millennium Development Goals have emanated from the UN Millennium Summit (September 2000). They consist of eight goals in the field of human development like reduction of extreme poverty and hunger (goal 1), reducing child mortality (goal 4), but also policy changes by industrialised countries in matters like aid, trade, debt, and technology transfers (goal 8). The time target for attaining most of the goals is 2015.

5. Development Cooperation

Of course, all this foreign currency was meant to fight poverty and to be invested in the country's development. So what went wrong? Much has been said and written in answer to this question, and there is no need to repeat those good analyses here. What I want to point at now is just this misfit imagination that came from faraway places together with the foreign intervention. The paradigms, the themes, the foci, and the spearheads of the donor policies—the imagination appears under different names—all have one thing in common: they confuse cause with result. In order to develop, these policies say that we must have democracy, good governance, gender equity, human rights, social justice, institutional capacity, and the list goes on. Yet we should take note that all these very pleasant conditions in the societies of rich countries have been acquired as a *result* of economic development. The social/institutional conditions in Europe and the United States at the beginnings of their journey towards the greater comforts of today were quite the opposite of all these fine accomplishments. They remained so for a very long time, and to be honest, they are still not perfect today.

So if democracy and gender equity are more of an accompanying result than of a precondition, then what really is the cradle of development? This is a question to be answered by the people of a society themselves. When the people have found some answers, then and only then can foreign aid come in and leave its imagination at home. This does not mean we should not try to foster the aspects of greater human culture like democracy and equity in any society, and let's begin with our own. This is to make us understand that the beginnings of development require other qualities, and self-determination is their common trait.

Having discussed the imagination of the policies, let us now turn to the actual reality of development relations. These relations of good intent are not free of strain. No doubt true meeting of hearts takes place and bonds of rich intercultural exchange are fastened. However, for this to happen we do not have to wait for the situation where one must help the other. What this happy merrymaking really should be about is remedying the lack of a self-empowered economy of the one. But unfortunately, in this dance of pity with the poor it is the other who always takes the lead.

We do not need deep analyses of the sector's practice in order to make our point. We just need to look at complicated and time-consuming procedures that donors make beneficiaries pass before they can access the benefit. We just need to consider the conditions donors dictate to those whose life's conditions are already precarious. And we just need to see the cumbersome reports that must be written for donors' satisfaction in the time of those who must still satisfy their basic needs. Development workers of third world countries have become so trained to dance to the donor's tune that they have forgotten how to make their own steps. In fact, what they call the way to do their work is really quite conditioned by decades of cultural anthropology, geographic sociology, social psychology, and charitable theology developed at institutions that are not their own. And really, people just want to plough their fields, feed their children, and live as agents of their lives and not as subjects in some academic study.

Need for development aid comes from a structural lack of material means and methods. To conclude that this implies the better moral status of the richer donor is a primitive belief that lends god-like status, not to sun and moon, but to money and technology. Let people with a moral mission don the clerical cloak and not disguise themselves in secular apparel.

As I stated earlier, the beginnings of development require the trait of self-determination. Now let me be more specific. When speaking of developing the structures of one's life and land, what people must essentially acquire is the skill to solve the many problematic situations that continually occur in life. This problem-solving skill that is pro-active, is lead by self-formulated goals, and seeks to maximise control is what we call the skill of management and possibly is more of an attitude than a skill.

A housewife who steers her household or a CEO who presides over a multinational corporation basically fulfill the same task: they both command activities towards the attainment of self-declared goals by way of self-designed strategies. They must do this in an environment that is ever dynamic and unpredictable. It is this manager's skill or attitude that must either be already there or must be fostered first when taking on development projects with or without foreign aid. Equipped with that skill, as people go about solving their problems and managing their lives, deficiencies of material, money, technology, or information will manifest. It is only in this context that aid from outside can come in. The problem-solving strategy itself must be the people's own. Studies done at distant desks may inform or may confuse, but they can never determine the strategies for the people on the ground. And another mystification I care to dismantle is the belief that foreign aid and the projects it supports are structural in any way. Aid from outside, by the very virtue of being foreign, always is ad hoc and limited in its reach. Life-sustaining structures can only be the result of a self-empowered approach by people who want to help themselves.

It is right that project money must be accounted for. But the only party that needs to check the boxes for satisfactory implementation and result is the one that must experience the satisfaction. And speaking of money, there is this relationship between donor and receiver, be they governments or non-governmental organisations (NGOs). As said before, to have enriching friendships between people of countries and cultures we do not need to ride the ticket of development. For that we can create ample opportunities in other ways. From the point of view of development itself, the bilateral bond does not bring any added value. In fact, knowing the country of origin only brings along the risk of cultural domination and donor intimidation together with the aid.

In the setup of development projects, large or small, full space must be given to the party that seeks development and his own self-chosen approach. And therefore we must disconnect the direct link between giver and receiver, implying that the donor should remain anonymous. This would require structures where financial flows from donor countries are gathered at neutral points. From these points they can be dispensed in decentralising movements down to the smallest local project. People from random countries must transparently manage such institutions. They should have no particular relation with the countries from where the money comes or where it goes. Management and staff should purely become employed by virtue of their skills and not for politics. And it is best to change personnel on a regular basis in order to avoid bonding between the parties. An institution set up in this way is neither bilateral nor multilateral; the politics of donor countries does not come into the picture.

To confront developing countries with a multitude of donor countries that each bring along their own policies is some remnant of past ties. From the point of view of efficient development cooperation, this does not make sense at all. To confound the treasuring of relations, for old time's sake or future business, with the moral stand that the rich should support the poor is entangling good intentions with wrong organisation. Has not our discourse at least surpassed the glorification of colonial possession and replaced it with the values of intercultural respect? So let us compose the structures of our aid in harmony with the good sounding words of that new ideal.

Surely, the disbursement of development assistance will need criteria. Like a bank will look at secure chances of returns on capital loaned, so an institution disbursing money for development aid will need to go by some measure of expected result. How do we go about this when we do not want to repeat the same mistake of imposing external standards on people's internal projects? The beneficiary must define standards and measure points for evaluation in his own terminology and on his own terms. But he must also show the prospect of concrete results—and that is results for real people—that can be objectively measured and seen by everyone; that will be the sound and common basis for extending aid in a variety of situations.

6. Concerns of International Economic Policy—Distinguish Three Spheres, Separate Three Strategies

In this chapter, the last of this book, I reorganise some of the material discussed before. With the focus on deeply unequal strength between the economies of this world I want to make some clear distinctions there where policies are often wrongly confounded. With balance of power in mind—not between few economic power blocks but one that allows for all cultures of economy, however small, to co-exist—I address three spheres of international relations that each requires its separate approach.

The first sphere is the one where nations and a large part of their population are faced with extreme poverty, where people have no peace, no prospects, and will not be able to start off in life without concerted policy efforts by those who govern them and practical aid of others who care for them. It is really the sense of responsibility of the own local and national policymakers that must make the change. Most of this squalor and despair can be cleared away with the nation's own means. It is often not huge material help that is needed. A change of soft structures like better cooperation, less bureaucracy, more efficient management, and an increased sense of mutual responsibility will already work wonders. Small improvements of physical living conditions and other necessary infrastructure can at these levels of misery often give people at least a beginning of hope.[1] Really, in this sphere of extreme poverty, charitable help from outside may even prove to be a hindrance for the country's own class of well-to-do to take up responsibility for their fellow citizens, and foreign policy intervention may freeze the initiative of local and national governments. Certainly, the efforts must be continued over a long period of time, and if, and only if, aid from abroad is seen to be absolutely indispensable, then it should come as a support attached to the inherent efforts, without much trumpeting its foreign name.

---

1.   See Appendix E on "Agricultural Policies and Poverty."

The second sphere is the one of low development of nations and their people. It is not only a poor people's right to obtain better living conditions and growth of opportunities, but in a world that chooses to be economically interdependent, also the rich prefer a better balance. Economy thrives by virtue of circulation, and more participants means more economy to circulate. Development, it has already been said more than once, cannot be financed by loans and bonds. Whether it is education or health or housing or roads or seeds for crops or transport infrastructure or capacity building for institutions or improved technology for industry, when the denominator is development, nations and their people must not be asked to repay with or without interest. Only when a country has arrived at more advanced stages of development, large commercial credits can start to come in. Capital for production or trade that goes to the market and will make a profit can be loaned at conditions that seem fit to the level of development, that is, more or less concessional. But non-market strategies of development, like in the field of health or education, should always be done with money that is free. In Part I we already saw that banking is one job and development is another and that creating debts is not a fit policy when still growing up.

So, in international relations, who will take care of this? It really is more a matter of the developing country's will than of the donor country's conditions. Industrialised countries, whose chosen lifestyles command internationalisation and whose economies need globalisation of markets, cannot afford to leave part of this world undeveloped. They literally have no choice and must contribute to the levelling of playing fields. Developing countries should come to understand that the business of development really is a buyer's market. With true development as their argument, it is up to them to set the price.

Now the third sphere of international economic cooperation is the one between nations of mature economies. That is, economies that have seen long periods of growth, that seem to be able to overcome passing periods of recession from within their own vitality, and whose people, on the whole, have their basic needs and even more fulfilled. This book did not set out to address policies between mature economies, but as somehow we have arrived at this point, I will use the opportunity to make just one remark. Right at the outset of this book we observed that all national economic policies seem to have declared growth as their official creed. Now let us see what happens when all nations bring this growth agenda to the international stage. What—as all nations together—are we then really striving for? Is it ever-continuing global growth? The best answer to this question is deep silence, so everyone can introspect and find his own truth.

Francis Fukuyama[2] may have seen the end of history in democratic societies and liberal economies, but interdependent economy says there still is some more to go. When unflinching focus on fulfilling the needs of life will have replaced the political economy of growth, the history of nations indeed may end, and civilisation of mankind can finally begin.

---

2.   Francis Fukuyama in his *The End of History and the Last Man (1992)* argues that liberal democracy, the only socio-political paradigm left after the fall of communism, marks the end of history. There is no further development that can improve on this, so he says.

Epilogue

This book has attempted to approach world imbalances from the point of view of the economic discipline. It tried to distinguish between common sense and nonsense in economic thinking and the ensuing policies. But let us make no mistake; imbalances do not come from not understanding the principles of the economic discipline as such. The challenge is not to understand economics as if it were a high science for academics only. The economic challenge for everyone is to provide for life with the assets that one has. Successful economy, therefore, is understanding the nature of the challenge and the efficient use of assets that are available.

At the outset of Europe's economic rise, the origin of today's capitalised world economy, the challenge was to increase production in order to fulfill the needs of growing populations while at the same time lifting the quality of life above mere slaving for survival. The assets Europe had in the seventeenth and eighteenth centuries were the movement of the Enlightenment, the Industrial Revolution, and the world seas to sail. These assets have been successfully employed to further growth of production, consumption, and capital accumulation. And not only could we meet Europe's challenges of the time, but as an unexpected bonus we can now also fulfill the needs of the people of all continents.

Adapting to a new environment is a basic law of survival, and to forget this primitive rule will certainly destroy civilisation. Growth is not anymore the challenge of today; it has become a piece of cake. Today's accomplished technology produces more than we can consume, and comforts come to us in futuristic features. The new challenge now is to redistribute economic opportunity—a new skill we still must train. But we have new assets too, and let us put them to good use: the awareness that policies should be for people—we call it democracy; and the vision of world peace—we created the United Nations.

The principles of interdependent economy are mere tools to meet the economic challenge of today. May people take up these tools and construct their lives with the assets of the world we all share.

APPENDIX A

Dam Projects in India and Tibet

The Dams of the Narmada River, India

www.narmada.org.

...The total project of dam construction on the Narmada River (1312 km long) comprises thirty big dams, 135 medium dams, and 3000 small dams. Of the big dams, Sardar Sarovar Project (SSP) and Narmada Sagar Project (NSP) are the two mega dams.

Popular protest by the people of the Narmada valley began in 1985–1986 when people had to be displaced by the SSP. Since then the struggle has spread to encompass other major dams in various stages of planning and construction. The Tawa and Bargi dams were completed in 1973 and 1989 respectively, and people who were affected have organised post-displacement to demand their rights.

Opponents of the dam believe that the assumptions of the Narmada Development Plan are unjust and iniquitous, and the cost-benefit analysis is grossly inflated in favour of building the dams.... They also believe that water and energy can be provided to the people of the Narmada valley, Gujarat, and other regions through alternative technologies and planning processes that can be socially just and economically and environmentally sustainable.... The questions that arise in the Narmada struggle challenge the dominant model of development...that holds out the chimerical promise of material wealth through modernisation, but perpetuates an iniquitous distribution of resources, and wreaks social and environmental havoc.

Worldwide protest against the Narmada dam project caused the World Bank to withdraw from it in 1993 after it had supported it with a U.S. $450 million loan pledge in 1985. The remaining balance of U.S. $200 million was subsequently cancelled. Such a revert on action is unique in the history of the World Bank!

In June of 2003 the International Accountability Project, California (U.S.A.) called on the World Bank to take remedial action against the undesirable effects of the dam construction in their letter annex report (*The Impact of the 2002 Submergence on Housing and Land Rights in the Narmada Valley*, published by Habitat International Coalition). In particular the letter points out the total lack of rehabilitation for thousands of displaced families....

Dams in Tibet, Province of Kham

"Tibetans to lose land for Chinese dams," *Tibetan Review*, Delhi, June 2003.

...In order to generate electricity and supply drinking water to Chinese cities, China is to build seven dams in Barkham and nearby counties of Ngaba Tibetan Autonomous Prefecture (TAP), in the traditional Tibetan province of Kham...China displaced sixty peasant families in Gonjo County of Chamdo Prefecture to Nyingtri prefecture within the TAR. The report did not specify the purpose of the displacement, which was carried out upon the pain of a fine of 70,000 yuan for disobeying the pack up order. Compensation was said to have been promised but never delivered. The farmers could not earn a living in Nyingtri and many went to Lhasa to seek work....

www.tibet.com.

...The proposed U.S. $250 million dam on Megoe Lake in south-eastern Tibet is located on a tributary of the Yangtze River. The lake is a sacred monument of this world's natural heritage and of great spiritual value to the Tibetan people. The electricity that will be produced by the project will benefit Chinese industry but none of the Tibetans who will be displaced and compulsorily resettled....

APPENDIX B

Mining in the South

Investment in Mining in the South

"Mining, Murder and Mayhem: The Impact of the Mining Industry in the South" by Danny Kennedy (*Third World Resurgence*, no. 93, May 1998). The article contains a case study of the Grasberg Gold Mine in Irian Jaya (West Papua), Indonesia. To access the entire article see: www.twnside.org.sg/title/mine-cn.htm.

...How big is the problem? Sixty percent of foreign direct investment in Africa last year was in the mineral extraction sector. Spending on exploration for metals in Latin America rose from $200 million in 1991 to $1,770 million in 1997. The situation in the Philippines optimises this expense. Since the Philippines national government created its GATT-consistent (precursor of the WTO, ed.) investment regimes and new mining laws in the mid-1990s, over 25% of that country has fallen prey to foreign-owned exploration or extraction concessions. The economic model is clearly one of extraction and export to core countries—not for enriching producing nations....

APPENDIX C

The Informal Sector

Some Notions and Figures

"The Informal Economy: Large and Growing in Most Developing Countries" by Simeon Djankov. To access the entire article see: http://rru.worldbank.org/ Discussions/Topics/Topic18.aspx.

...The so-called informal sector is that part of economic activity where income goes unreported. As a consequence no state taxes are collected, nor is it accounted for in GDP figures. The majority of the activity is undoubtedly perfectly productive and economically justified, but always being illegal in some sorts, some activity may be criminal.

In Africa the informal economy is so large it is more like a parallel economy. On average the informal economy in Africa is estimated to have been 42% of GDP in 1999/2000. In Latin America, the average size of the informal economy was 41% of GDP. In transition countries the rates varied between 67.3% (Georgia) and 18.9% (the Slovak Republic). In Asia the range was from Thailand at 52.6% to Singapore with 13.1% and Japan with 11.3%. Even in European OECD countries the average was 18%.

The size of the informal labour market is especially hard to measure. "Underground" labour may consist of a second job after (or even during) regular working hours, informal economy work by individuals who do not participate in the official labour market, and employment of people (e.g., clandestine or illegal immigrants) who are not allowed to work in the official economy....

The Informal Sector in Latin America

www.cato.org/pubs/journal/cj17n1-8.html.

A seminal work on the informal sector and the socio-economic revolutionary impact it can have is *The Other Path* written under the leadership of Hernando de Soto (published 1986). The book analyses the informal sector in the Latin American reality from a classical liberal perspective.

APPENDIX D
Counting People's Wealth

Aggregated money wealth

The world standard to indicate a nation's economic production is to compute total added value in terms of monetary units. Instances of this are the income of citizens and profits of businesses. Gross National Product (GNP) or Gross Domestic Product (GDP) are examples of the indicators most frequently used in this system.

Human Development

Since 1990, the Human Development Reports (HDR), published by the United Nations Development Programme (UNDP), have launched new indicators that rank a nation's level of development by counting people's money income as well as by taking measure of qualities like health (life expectancy) and education (adult literacy and enrolment in the educational system). New indicators are constantly developed, such as on aspects like gender equity, food security, or access to information and communication. The indicators of the HDRs draw the attention of policymakers to the diverse aspects of human life and thereby say that economic development and human development must be interdependent parts of policy.

Gross National Happiness in Bhutan

The official development policy in Bhutan is to achieve increase not of its Gross National Product but of its Gross National Happiness (GNH). "We are in search of a balance between economic growth and preservation of tradition and spirituality," says Dasho Ugyen Tshering, Deputy Minister of Foreign Affairs of Bhutan (*Volkskrant*, 5 January, 2001). The concept of GNH as the lead for Bhutan's development policy is, however, not a quantifiable indicator like the GNP. It is a development philosophy made operational through the four platforms of economic development, environmental preservation, cultural promotion, and good governance.

For more information see:
www.dop.gov.bt
travelbhutan.tripod.com/druk.html
www.bhutanstudies.org.bt/publications/gnh/gnh.htm
www.bhutannewsonline.com/economy.html

APPENDIX E
Agricultural Policies and Poverty

Subsidies in Rich Countries

Strong subsidising in industrial countries of their already mature and well-developed agricultural sector and agribusiness is already much documented. The article by Devinder Sharma "WTO and Agriculture: The Great Trade Robbery" gives a graphic description of the situation. To access the entire article see: http://www.mindfully.org/WTO/2003/Trade-Robery-WTO-Sharma2sep03.htm.

…Rich countries subsidise agribusiness by allowing them to buy very cheap, with the government then making up some of the differences with direct payment to farmers.

So much so that the recipients of the U.S. agricultural subsidies in 2001 also included Ted Turner and David Rockefeller—no wonder, the CNN continues to stifle the voice of the developing countries' farmers. The richest man in the United Kingdom, the Duke of Westminster, who owns about 55,000 hectares of farm estates, receives an average subsidy of 300,000 pound sterlings as direct payments, and in addition gets 350,000 pounds a year for the 1,200 dairy cows he owns.

It certainly is an unequal world, and perhaps the most debasing and demeaning of all the world's inequalities is the manner in which the cattle in the rich countries are pampered at the cost of several hundred million farmers in the developing world. When I first compared the life of the western cow with that of the third World farmer, I didn't realise that this would hit the sensibilities of at least some of the economists and policy makers. It has now been worked out that the EU provides a daily subsidy of U.S. $2.7 per cow, and Japan provides three times more at U.S. $8, whereas half of India's 1000 million people live on less than $2 a day.…

Mismanagement of Food Stocks in India

A third of the world's estimated 800 million hungry live in India—that is 320 million people. This situation persists in spite of food stocks of 38 million tonnes in 2003 and 65 million tonnes in 2002. That India does not need the Millennium Goals Aid Programme or foreign currency to feed its people becomes clear from the following analysis. "GM Industry and Science: Busy Exploiting Hunger," article by Devinder Sharma, October 2003. To access the entire article see: http://www.mindfully.org/GE/2003/Exploiting-Hunger-GM-Industry3oct03.htm.

...In 2002–03, nearly 17 million tonnes from the unmanageable food surplus has been diverted for exports, and that too at a price that was actually meant for people living below the poverty line...A report of the Standing Committee of Parliament had estimated that the government was spending Rs 62,000 million every year to maintain these food stocks.

...Shouldn't the politician-industry-scientist trio impress upon the government the folly of spending Rs. 62,000 million in storing the grains and not spending the same amount on its distribution? Couldn't the industry come forward to help the nation fight the scourge of mankind? After all, there is no shortage of food....

Devinder Sharma is a well-known Indian journalist and writer. He researches on policy issues concerning sustainable agriculture, biodiversity and intellectual property rights, environment and development, food security and poverty, biotechnology and hunger, and the implications of the free trade paradigm for developing countries.

Bibliography

Books and Papers

Caufield, Catherine. *Masters of Illusion: The World Bank and the Poverty of Nations.* London: Pan Books, 1998. To order see: www.frontlist.com/detail/0805028757.

Clay, Jason. *World Agriculture and the Environment: A commodity-by-commodity guide to impacts and practices.* Covelo, California: Island Press, 2004.

Fukuyama, Francis. *The End of History and the Last Man.* Old Tappan, New Jersey: Penguin, 1992.

Hertz, Noreena. *The Silent Takeover: Global Capitalism and the Death of Democracy.* London: Arrow, 2002.

Michel, Andrée, Floch, *Citoyennes Militairement Incorrectes.* Paris: l'Harmattan, 1999. See : http://1libertaire.free.fr/AMichel04.html.

Michel, Andrée. *Surarmement Pouvoir Démocratie.* Paris: l'Harmattan, 1996.

Ormerod, Paul. *The Death of Economics.* London: Faber and Faber, 1994.

Oxfam. *Cultivating poverty: The Impact of US cotton subsidies on Africa.* Oxfam Briefing Paper no.30. Available from: http://www.oxfam.org.uk/what_we_do/issues/trade/bp30_cotton.htm.

Oxfam. *The Great EU Sugar Scam: How Europe's sugar regime is devastating livelihoods in the developing world.* Oxfam Briefing Paper no. 27. Available from: http://www.oxfam.org.uk/what_we_do/issues/trade/bp27_sugar.htm.

Sharma, Devinder. *GATT to WTO: Seeds of Despair.* New Delhi: Konark Publishers Pvt. Ltd and The Book Review literary trust, 1995.

Sharma, Devinder: *In The Famine Trap.* London: The Ecological Foundation and UK Food Group, 1997.

Sharma, Devinder: *WTO and Agriculture: The Great Trade Robbery*. New Delhi: Forum for Biotechnology & Food Security. Paper presented at a debate on international politics entitled "Agrarhandel—Stolperstein Für Die WTO?" with Renate Kunast, Minister for Agriculture, Germany, at the Legislative Assembly, Berlin, September 2, 2003.

de Soto, Hernando. *The Mystery of Capital: Why Capitalism Triumphs in the West and Fails Everywhere Else*. New York: Basic Books, 2000.

de Soto, Hernando. *The Other Path*. New York: Basic Books, 1989.

Web Sites

On development

www.ild.org.pe. Instituto de Libertad y Democracia (ILD). Hernando de Soto is currently President of the ILD, headquartered in Lima, Peru.

www.oxfam.org.uk. Oxfam Great Britain is a development, relief, and campaigning organisation. Oxfam publishes on issues of U.S. and E.U. agricultural subsidies that cultivate poverty in developing countries.

www.newint.org. New Internationalist Publications reports on issues of world poverty and inequality to focus attention on the unjust relationship between the powerful and the powerless in both rich and poor nations and to debate and campaign for the radical changes necessary if the basic material and spiritual needs of all are to be met.

travelbhutan.tripod.com/druk.html. A web site on a recent discussion (2004) of the Gross National Happiness concept of Bhutan.

www.bhutanstudies.org.bt/publications/gnh/gnh.htm. A collection of papers on Bhutan's Gross National Happiness by Bhutanese and western authors (1999).

On food and trade

www.dsharma.org/aboutme.htm. Devinder Sharma, journalist, writer, thinker, and analyst of policies of food trade and food technology.

www.twnside.org.sg/index.htm. Web site of the Third World Network on Trade issues and rules and the WTO.

www.ictsd.org/weekly/index.htm. *Bridges: A Weekly Trade News Digest* bridging the trade and sustainable development communities.

www.fairfood.org. Fairfood is an organisation in the Netherlands that informs on hunger in Third World countries and food trade policies. (Web site in Dutch.)

On international finance and debt

www.attac.org/index.htm. International ATTAC was created in Paris in 1998 for democratic control of financial markets and their institutions.

www.waronwant.org/?lid=5441. On the Tobin tax.

www.eurodad.org/. Eurodad is a network of European development NGOs working for national economic and international financing policies that achieve poverty eradication and the empowerment of the poor.

www.osjspm.org/debt.htm. Office for Social Justice: a Web page on the debt crisis of the Archdiocese of St. Paul and Minneapolis, U.S.A.

webhost.bridgew.edu/jhayesboh/debt.htm. A Web page on International Debt Relief.

www.flora.org/flora/archive/mai-not/;   www.globalissues.org/TradeRelated/ MAI.asp;   www.globalpolicy.org/socecon/bwi-wto/oecd-mai.htm.   Web sites on the Multilateral Agreement on Trade (MAI).

People's organisations

www.narmada.org. The Friends of the Narmada valley and its people present the perspective of grassroots people's organisations on the building of the dams in the Narmada valley, India.

www.50years.org. U.S. network for global economic justice.

www.worldhunger.org. An online publication of the World Hunger Education Service (WHES).

www.taxpayer.net. A non-partisan budget watchdog (U.S.A.).

International institutions

www.undp.org. United Nations Development Programme. The UNDP has published the Human Development Reports (HDR) since 1990.

www.wto.org. The World Trade Organization (WTO) is the only global international organisation dealing with the rules of trade between nations. At its heart are the WTO agreements, negotiated and signed by the bulk of the world's trading nations and ratified in their parliaments.

www.worldbank.org. The World Bank Group's mission is to fight poverty and improve the living standards of people in the developing world. It is a development Bank which provides loans, policy advice, technical assistance and knowledge sharing services to low and middle income countries to reduce poverty.

www.imf.org. The IMF is an organisation of 184 countries, working to foster global monetary cooperation, secure financial stability, facilitate international trade, promote high employment and sustainable economic growth, and reduce poverty.

www.europa.eu.int/comm/trade/issues/global/development/index_en.htm. Web site on trade and development policies and issues of the European Union.

978-0-595-33152-9
0-595-33152-1

www.ingramcontent.com/pod-product-compliance
Lightning Source LLC
Chambersburg PA
CBHW030840180526
45163CB00004B/1395